W9-BSY-669

Boundless Heart

Boundless Heart

*The Buddha's Path of Kindness, Compassion,
Joy, and Equanimity*

CHRISTINA FELDMAN

Shambhala

BOULDER

2017

Shambhala Publications, Inc.
4720 Walnut Street
Boulder, Colorado 80301
www.shambhala.com

9 8 7 6 5 4 3 2

Printed in the United States of America

⊗ This edition is printed on acid-free paper that meets the
American National Standards Institute Z39.48 Standard.
♻ This book was printed on 30% post-consumer recycled paper.
For more information please visit www.shambhala.com.

Shambhala Publications is distributed worldwide
by Penguin Random House, Inc., and its subsidiaries.

Designed by Dean Bornstein

LIBRARY OF CONGRESS CATALOGING-IN-PUBLICATION DATA

Names: Feldman, Christina, author.
Title: Boundless heart: the Buddha's path of kindness, compassion,
joy, and equanimity / Christina Feldman.
Description: First edition. | Boulder, Colorado: Shambhala Publications, Inc.,
[2017] | Includes bibliographical references.
Identifiers: LCCN 2016024064 | ISBN 9781611803730 (pbk.: acid-free paper)
Subjects: LCSH: Spiritual life—Buddhism. | Religious life—Buddhism.
| Kindness—Religious aspects—Buddhism. | Compassion—Religious
aspects—Buddhism. | Joy—Religious aspects—Buddhism.
Classification: LCC BQ5560 .F45 2017 | DDC 294.3/444—dc23
LC record available at https://lccn.loc.gov/2016024064

Contents

Boundless Heart

Introduction

The Landscape and Embodiment of Liberation

There is no greater love than the immeasurable friendliness that can embrace all beings, all events, and all experiences with unshakeable kindness. There is no compassion greater than the fearless heart that can turn toward suffering and pain, tremble with empathy, and live with the commitment to end the causes of anguish. There is no greater happiness than inwardly generated joy and peace. There is no equanimity more unshakeable than the profound poise of the liberated heart that can meet the world of ungraspable conditions and events without being shattered.

Threaded through the entirety of the Buddha's pathway of awakening are the teachings on cultivating the boundless heart—immeasurable kindness, compassion, joy, and equanimity. These qualities are referred to as the *brahma viharas. Brahma* refers to the sublime or noble tenor of these qualities; *vihara* originally comes from the word for "monastery," or the place we abide and make our home. We are encouraged, whether standing or walking, sitting or lying down, whenever we are awake to make kindness, compassion, joy, and equanimity the home of our heart. This is the noblest way of living in this world here and now.

The brahma viharas are relational qualities. They are the foundation of all respectful, healthy, and dignified societies, communities, families, and relationships. Kindness, compassion, joy, and equanimity are virtues, wholesome qualities that are the foundation of all ethical thought, speech, and action. They are qualities to be cultivated in all moments, in the midst of all the conditions and events that touch our lives, the lovely and the unlovely, the challenging and the easeful. They are pathways of awakening and liberation encouraging us to investigate anguish and its origins and to cultivate the path to the end of struggle and discontentment. These ennobling qualities are also the embodied expression of the awakened heart describing the deepest emotional and psychological freedom and maturity of a human being. When these qualities are brought to fruition, they are described as immeasurable, without conditions, and unshakeable. They are the landscape and embodiment of liberation.

The interwoven nature of the brahma viharas is beautifully described by the teacher Longchenpa, a prominent teacher in the Nyingma school of Tibetan Buddhism in the fourteenth century.

> Out of the soil of friendliness grows the beautiful bloom of
> compassion,
> Watered by the tears of joy,
> Sheltered beneath the cool shade of the tree of equanimity.[1]

Kindness, compassion, joy, and equanimity are a family of qualities that support, strengthen, nourish, and balance one another. Immeasurable kindness teaches us a way of being in this world that is no longer defined by ideas of friends and enemies, by likes and dislikes, preferences and demands for reciprocation. Boundless friendliness is the root of compassion and protects it from despair and partiality. Kindness guards equanimity from falling into indifference.

Compassion protects kindness from falling into sentimentality or becoming only a state of elation, always recollecting the reality of the immensity of sorrow in the world. Compassion, rooted in kindness, becomes selfless and protects joy from forgetfulness. Compassion extends the remit of kindness and turns it into altruistic and healing action.

Joy is needed to temper the raw edges of sorrow and pain encountered as our hearts tremble in the face of sorrow and anguish. Joy brings ease and rest into our endeavors to bring the origins of suffering to an end. The joyful heart tempers pain and suffering with the remembering of that which is well and unbroken, even in the midst of distress, and guards the compassionate heart from being overwhelmed by sorrow.

Equanimity brings to kindness and compassion patience and steadiness; equanimity balances joy, protecting it from wandering into the emotional extremes of exuberance, just as joy softens and brings serenity to equanimity. Equanimity allows us to act without becoming preoccupied with the results and outcomes of our actions. It is a quality of strength and inner poise that allows us to respond to the world of experience without fear and hesitation.

A woman with many years of meditation practice said,

> I had listened to teachings on boundless friendliness, compassion, joy, and equanimity for years but never really knew what they meant until my daughter was admitted to the pediatric cancer ward when she was eight years old. All of the children on the ward were desperately ill and undergoing treatments that were hard to bear. Yet strangely, they formed a kind of family. When Sadie was admitted, the children who could immediately befriended her. They didn't spend time telling the story of their cancer. When any of them were really struggling, those who were able would visit and share a favorite toy. They could smile, laugh, and play; at times, there were many moments of genuine happiness. When any of them were discharged, the others celebrated. There was a curious poise evident in many of the children. They knew so much was out of their hands; they had so little control yet there was little rage or despair. They were some of the most present-moment-centered and receptive people I had ever met. I learned so much from these children and from my own daughter. The kindness, compassion, joy, and equanimity they embodied were lessons I needed to learn. They were the lessons that sustained us all in the darkest of times.

The experiential taste of the brahma viharas is not a stranger to us. Each of us has encountered moments of unhesitating friendliness, compassion, joy, and equanimity. At times we have been the recipients of these qualities—offered to us by loved ones and by strangers. Equally we have all known moments when we have responded to others with unreserved kindness and compassion. At times we unexpectedly encounter moments of profound appreciation and joy. In some of the most challenging moments of our lives we surprise ourselves with our capacity to be balanced and steady. These moments make a powerful imprint on our minds, revealing to us an inner potentiality and way of being in the world that is responsive and liberated. Too often these moments feel accidental, windows that open to an ennobled way of living that too easily seem to close again. Once more we find ourselves self-absorbed, fearful, and forgetful, lost in the preoccupations of our day. The moments of deepest distress and despair in our lives are the moments when kindness, compassion, joy, and equanimity are most prone to disappear, yet these are the moments when these qualities are our greatest allies and most needed.

The great genius of the Buddha's teaching was to build upon what we have already known and glimpsed in our lives. The brahma viharas are not an exotic import of transcendent states, unfamiliar to us, but are an invitation to train, develop, and nurture the seeds of kindness, compassion, joy, and equanimity that lie in each of our hearts. They are pathways that begin with acknowledging that these moments of unhesitating responsiveness do not need to be accidental or episodic encounters but, with dedication and cultivation, can become our home, the place our hearts abide. Our path does not begin with these qualities being immeasurable and unshakeable, but with their being elusive, unpredictable, and measured. We are aware of all of the moments we do not embody kindness, the moments we turn away from suffering, the moments of darkness when joy is forgotten, and the many moments of impulsiveness and reactivity in our lives when equanimity feels to be only a distant memory.

Rather than being discouraged by these many moments of forgetfulness—the times of anger, fear, despair, and reactivity—we come to recognize that this is the classroom in which the immeasurable capacities of our hearts are nurtured and cultivated. This is a present-moment recollection, a quality of mindfulness where we learn to cultivate kindness in the midst of harshness, compassion in the face of the seemingly impossible, joy in the midst of sorrow and darkness, and equanimity in the midst of the events of our lives that feel designed to unbalance us. This is not a path of postponement that waits for the ideal conditions and moments to be kind, compassionate, joyful, and balanced within. This is the nature of the immeasurable—it embraces all moments, events, and conditions. Kindness, compassion, joy, and equanimity can only be cultivated in the present, in our willingness to meet our life with a responsive and wise heart.

As a pathway of cultivation, the brahma viharas have several equally important aspects. Firstly the cultivation of kindness, compassion, joy, and equanimity reminds us of the altruistic heart of every contemplative journey. We do not engage in this challenging journey only for our own benefit. We commit ourselves to the cultivation of the brahma viharas for the benefit of those we love, those we struggle with, and those unknown to us. We are learning to widen our circle of concern and care to embrace all beings. Each one of us has our personal and unique story in this life to be honored and understood. We have our own measure of joy and sorrow, relatedness and loss, fear and trust. We all know what it is to experience pain and struggle, acceptance and rejection, hope and despair. The people we love, those we struggle with, and those unknown to us equally have their own personal and unique story, to be honored and understood. Kindness, compassion, joy, and equanimity are universal, inclusive, boundless—a naturalized abiding as immeasurable as the world of alienation and pain.

The brahma viharas offer us ways of embracing the vicissitudes of our life with grace, compassion, and understanding. Equally they encourage us to open our eyes and hearts and know that our story rests within the universal story of all. We look around ourselves and know that those we love, those we struggle with, and the many beings we have never met have their own measure of sorrow and joy. No one is exempt from loss, unwelcome change, uncertainty, and instability. We share with all the longings for happiness, acceptance, love, respect. We share with all the longings to be free from isolation, fear, and pain. This awareness does not diminish our personal experience but places us firmly in the family of all beings. The qualities of kindness, compassion, joy, and equanimity exclude no one—their cultivation is dedicated to the well-being, peace, and freedom of heart of all beings.

The cultivation of the brahma viharas is a training in intentionally inclining the heart toward emotional and psychological maturity and freedom, inclining the heart toward the possibility of befriending the moment, cultivating compassion, remembering joy, and placing our heart upon the steady ground of equanimity. Intention is the forerunner of our thoughts, words, and acts and all the ways we interface with the world. Intention has roots and is shaped by those roots. When intention is rooted in greed, hatred, or delusion, it will invariably manifest in impulsive reactivity and pain. The Buddha clearly recognized that greed, hatred, and confusion are the primary creators of struggle, fear, and emotional pain in our lives. They are deeply rooted habit patterns, taking us to places of alienation, shame, guilt, and despair that are far from where we wish to be, or how we wish to be. The intentional cultivation of kindness, joy, compassion, and equanimity is an antidote to the habits and impulses of greed, hatred, and delusion. They show us what it means to live an intentional life—embodying the values and aspirations we most deeply cherish, enabling us to touch the world with kindness, compassion, joy, and equanimity.

We are unlikely to wake in the morning and determine that this is a good day to be anxious, aversive, or judgmental. It can be deeply uncomfortable to see how impulsive and habitual many of our reactions and patterns are. Yet they are not a life sentence. Just because many of the habit patterns that create suffering have a long history does not mean they have an equally long future. They arise in the present and can be transformed in the present. Kindness, compassion, joy, and equanimity are a quality of mindfulness—the antidote to emotional and psychological habit. Experientially we come to understand that mindfulness and habit cannot coexist. Our times of being lost in habit are the most unconscious moments in our lives and often our moments of greatest reactivity and pain. Mindfulness has the effect of dissolving habit, one moment at a time. We learn we can through mindfulness and intention make an awakened heart our home and bring habit and reactivity to an end. We learn to incline our hearts toward the qualities that ennoble our lives and liberate the moment from fear, ill will, and confusion. This liberation is one of the most priceless gifts we can offer to ourselves and to another. It is a present-moment recollection, an ongoing renewal of intention, an awareness of where we are making our home or abiding in this moment—in that which causes suffering or in that which ends suffering.

The meditative practices of kindness, compassion, joy, and equanimity can be used, as we have more traditionally inherited them, as trainings in one-pointedness and concentration. A few simple phrases are used to capture and articulate both the intention and the direction of these abidings: "May I be peaceful; may you be peaceful. May I live with ease and with kindness; may you live with ease and with kindness." We learn to settle the mind within these phrases, and they become guardians of the mind/heart, protecting us from obsession, rumination, and proliferating thought, which so easily overwhelm us. The mind does not entertain more than one thought at a time, and we discover there is a choice about the thoughts we attend to. Obsession, rumination, and proliferation are a kind of psychological vandalism rarely delivering happiness, spaciousness, or peace. Their outcome tends to be increasingly closed feedback loops of narrative and thought that stifle the stillness, calm, and spaciousness that are the deepest potential of our mind. We discover we can learn to sustain the intentions and phrases of kindness, compassion, joy, and equanimity and cultivate a mind that is a true friend.

One of the jewels within the Buddha's path of wakening is this well-known teaching from the Honeyball Discourse: "What we frequently think about and dwell upon becomes the shape of our mind. The shape of our mind shapes our world of experience." We see in our own experience that if we repetitively dwell upon fear, ill will, or in obsession, we essentially get better at it and more prone to make those patterns our home. The patterns become almost our default mechanisms, creating and recreating distress and despair. If we frequently incline our hearts and make our homes intentionally within kindness, compassion, joy, and equanimity, these too become the shape of our mind, the homes we abide in, and shape our world of experience in a radically different way.

There is a basic formula that runs through the entire path of cultivating the brahma viharas:

> We abide, dwelling in kindness, compassion, joy and equanimity
> Pervading the entire world everywhere and equally with our hearts filled with
> kindness, compassion, joy and equanimity our hearts grown great, abundant, measureless, free from enmity and free from distress.

At the heart of the teaching of the brahma viharas there is the invitation to radically transform the shape of our hearts through understanding. In their deepest sense they are pathways of insight that bring confusion, greed, and hatred to an end, liberating the heart and establishing the mind in unshakeable and immeasurable kindness, compassion, joy, and equanimity. They teach us to live in this world fearlessly, how to be a true friend to ourselves and others, and to cultivate an inner abiding that is a true refuge. It is this aspect of transformative insight, liberating the heart through the brahma viharas, that I would like to focus upon in this book: to explore what it means for us to reframe kindness, compassion, joy, and equanimity so they are not seen as transient emotions or states but as embodiments of profound understanding and liberation that ennoble our lives and contribute to the healing of our world.

In the difficult world of India that the Buddha lived in twenty-six hundred years ago, with all its poverty, deprivation, and conflict, most of the existing meditative practices and traditions held the primary goal of transcendence. People understandably sought for a way out of a life that was so difficult and challenging, most often through asceticism, self-mortification, and striving. The body, mind, relationships, and society were frequently viewed as obstacles to liberation, to be disdained and overcome. A mystical, transcendent freedom was seen to lie elsewhere in some idealized other moment and place.

The Buddha himself followed many of these practices of self-denial and disconnection from the world only to discover they did not offer him the freedom and peace he so urgently sought. He discovered, as we discover, that it is not easy to quell the mind, heart, and body, which are our constant companions in this life. Nagarjuna, the great Indian sage, 150 C.E., was widely considered to be one of the most significant Buddhist teachers and founder of the Madhyamaka school of Tibetan Buddhism. He asked the question, "What do you do with a life that doesn't go away?" At the end of his fruitless pursuits to make life go away, the Buddha was a radical in his time in turning toward the moment, with all its imperfections, and taught that this very life is the classroom of our awakening. He turned toward his body and heart with the intention to understand distress and its causes and taking up the quest to understand what it would mean to be free within this life as it is. The Buddha did not abandon the quest for transcendence; he no longer sought the transcendence of the world, but to find transcendence within the confusion, suffering, and alienation of the world.

The patterns of fear, confusion, and aversion that featured so strongly in the time of the Buddha are equally prevalent in our world today. Conflict, hatred, suspicion, and greed scar our world. We may find ourselves pursuing ways to escape from this difficult life through addiction or dissociation. Rates of depression and self-harm are all too familiar in the lives of many as we lose confidence in our capacity to bring distress to an end and forget the genuine sense of the potentiality of our own hearts for freedom and peace. In confusion we are prone to heap pain upon pain through aversion and fear. As the Buddha put it, "what we frequently dwell upon, does this to our heart incline."

In looking closely at his heart and mind, the Buddha discovered a radically different way of being in this world in which fear and confusion could come to an end. He understood that to change our mind of the moment was to change our world of the moment and that suffering and fear only governed our hearts as long as we allowed ourselves to be intimidated by them. In turning toward everything we have been prone to abandon, with an intentional curiosity, kindness, and compassion, fear and dissociation can come to an end. The Buddha taught that the possibility of profound awakening and profound freedom is the heritage of every human being, to be discovered and understood within this very life.

Central to liberation the Buddha placed the pathways of kindness, compassion, joy, and equanimity. Cultivated wisely, they teach us to deeply understand the landscape of distress, the origins of distress, and the way to the end of distress and an unshakeable liberation of the heart. The brahma viharas show us a way to live in this world that is guided by the ennobling qualities of the heart that heal and liberate wherever they touch. The Buddha said he taught out of compassion for the suffering in the world. In cultivating the brahma viharas, we widen the circle of our concern and care, understanding we can be intentional participants in the healing and awakening of our world.

ONE

Immeasurable Kindness

In one of the earliest collections of the Buddha's teachings, the Sutta-nipāta, lies the jewel of the teaching—the Mettā-sutta, the discourse on immeasurable friendliness. The word *metta* draws on the Pali/Sanskrit word *mitta*, which translates as "friend." In turn *mitta* draws on an earlier Sanskrit word *mit* that translates as "growing fat with kindness" or "spreading out"—spreading out in friendliness to the world.

The Metta Sutta

To reach the state of peace
One skilled in the good should be
Capable and upright,
Easy to speak to and straightforward,
Of gentle nature and not proud,
Contented and easily supported,
Living lightly and having few duties,
Wise and with senses calmed,
Not arrogant and without greed for supporters,
And should not do the least thing that the wise
Would reproach them for.
(One should reflect in this way:)
"May all beings be happy and secure;
May all beings be happy-minded.
Whatever living beings there may be,
whether weak or strong,
Tall, large, medium, or short, small or big,
Seen or unseen, near or distant,

Born or to be born,
May they, without exception, all be happy-minded.
Let no one despise another
Or deceive anyone anywhere,
Let no one through anger or hatred
Wish for another's suffering."
As a mother would risk her own life
To protect her child, her only child,
So for all beings one should
Guard one's boundless heart.
With boundless friendliness for the whole world should one
Cultivate a boundless heart,
In all directions,
Without obstruction, without hate and without ill will,
Standing or walking, sitting or lying down,
Whenever one is awake,
May one stay with this recollection.
This is called the best and most sublime way of dwelling in this
    world.
One who is virtuous, endowed with insight,
Not clinging to wrong view,
And having overcome all passion for sensual pleasure,
Will not come to lie in a womb again.[1]

The four immeasurable qualities of kindness, compassion, joy, and equanimity should not be seen as linear or hierarchical, yet metta is the only one of these qualities that in the early collection of teachings merits its own dedicated discourse. It is seen to be the foundation of an ethical life, of words, thoughts, and acts of integrity. It is understood to be the necessary foundation of all ennobling qualities, including compassion, joy, and equanimity. It is said to be the necessary foundational attitude underlying all meditative development. Metta is not described as emotion or a transient state, but as an abiding—the home where our hearts and minds dwell. It is an attitudinal commitment brought to all moments of experience. Cultivating our capacity for boundless kindness opens the door to the boundlessness of compassion, joy, and equanimity. This involves a radical shift in our understanding and way of being present in all moments and rests upon a committed intention and practice. This book will initially give more attention to the cultivation of metta, not because it is more significant than compassion, joy, and equanimity, but because it is the indispensable foundation of an awakened heart.

With this teaching the Buddha describes a way of being in the world, in all moments, all circumstances, with a mind abiding in a boundless kindness in which greed, confusion, and ill will have come to an end. It is an all-inclusive befriending, a fearless kindness rooted in mindfulness and insight. *Metta* is also a verb—"befriending." We learn to befriend ourselves, all of the people who come into our lives—the difficult and the lovely. We learn to befriend all events and circumstances—the challenging and the lovely.

The Buddha recognized, as we recognize, the toxic power of ill will. Hatred, aversion, and fear fracture our communities, our societies, and our world. Historically and today, ill will creates wars and conflict, oppression, violence, and prejudice, and the suffering scars our lives and world. Ill will is not an abstract concept. Each one of us knows the pain of receiving ill will through the thoughts, words, or acts of another. Judgment, blame, harshness, rejection, condemnation, and suspicion leave a powerful imprint on our hearts and minds. We equally know the pain of being gripped by inwardly generated ill will when we judge, condemn, or are harsh to another. We know too the damage done through inwardly directed ill will—the all-too-familiar sniping voice of the inner critic and judge that undermines our well-being and happiness.

As an insight practice, the cultivation of metta—boundless friendliness—is directed toward uprooting the deeply embedded psychological and emotional pattern of ill will or aversion. Aversion has many faces—irritation, impatience, jealousy, blame, guilt, hatred, belittlement, disdain, and contempt. We feel the ripples of these patterns of emotional turmoil and ill will in our own minds. We see the ripples of aversion in the world around us when ill will becomes collective. The pain of being disenfranchised, disempowered, and abandoned through collective ill will is evident in our societies. The outcome is always the same—pain, separation, fragmentation, alienation, and harm. As the Vietnamese teacher Thich Nhat Hanh put it, "Anger and hatred are the materials from which hell is made."

From a Buddhist psychological perspective, ill will is rooted in fear—the fear of loss, the fear of harm.

When our hearts are gripped by fear, we create the sense of "other" that we abandon, flee from, or attack. The "other" may be simply the person who annoys us with restlessness when we want calm, the unwanted person trying to sell us new windows, the person in front of us in line impeding our progress. The "other" may be whole groups of people we condemn, mistrust, or judge. The many forms of prejudice that scar our world cannot survive without this aversive mechanism that creates the "other," in turn fueling mistrust, separation, and fear.

We feel the whispers and the powerful surges of ill will in our bodies, in our thoughts, and in our reactions. They move though our minds, our speech, and our acts. The Buddha refers to ill will as a poison that sickens us and leaves a powerful footprint upon the world. Aversion leaches joy and happiness from our hearts and life, bringing bleakness and alienation and triggering obsessive thinking. Aversion sets in motion downward spirals of depression and debilitating anxiety. There is little that can gladden a heart gripped by ill will. There is little room for joy, appreciation, or peace when the heart sinks beneath the weight of ill will. We feel the residues of ill will echoing in our hearts in regret, shame, and guilt. The momentum of aversion is to reject, to avoid, to annihilate, to get rid of, and to create distance between ourselves and the "other."

Aversion propels us into agitated behavior as we try to "fix" or rid ourselves of the people, events, and conditions we are convinced are the source of our unhappiness. Aversion is a habit pattern that can become so naturalized we cease to notice its effect upon our hearts and lives.

We may look back on our day and realize how often we have heard the voice of complaint, the eyes that highlight only the imperfect, and the numerous acts of avoidance we have engaged in. This awareness may be uncomfortable, yet it is the first step in sensitizing our hearts to the toxicity of ill will. Rather than inviting judgment or shame, it is an awareness that can be the beginning of a profound commitment to no longer consenting to aversion governing our hearts and committing ourselves to a life guided by immeasurable kindness.

We may be tempted to justify aversion—we tell ourselves that in a competitive, agitated, demanding world, aversion is the way we make ourselves heard or effect the changes we want. We tell ourselves that the small moments of irritation or impatience are inconsequential. We do not always see that the small ripples of aversion are of the same nature as the tsunamis of hatred and ill will that create and re-create suffering in life, inwardly and outwardly. A teacher within the Tibetan tradition taught:

> Do not take lightly small misdeeds,
> Believing they can do no harm;
> Even a tiny spark of fire
> Can set alight a mountain.[2]

At times the "others" that are created and solidified through aversion are aspects of our own being we disdain, judge, or fear: parts of our body, an illness, a chronic pain we fear and turn away from. We can be masters in the art of self-condemnation—disdaining ourselves and forming views of ourselves that are constructed on the foundations of self-hatred. We can have aversion for aversion, telling ourselves that a better or more spiritual person would not experience such ill will, which becomes a base for further self-judgment about our imperfections and inadequacies. We tell ourselves we should be a better person, yet we feel imprisoned by our own habit patterns and feel helpless in the face of them. We may have emotions of jealousy, contempt, or anxiety we feel ashamed of and turn them into the "other" we reject or endeavor to annihilate. The "other" is turned into an enemy within ourselves that we fear and condemn. The underlying narrative in aversion is about nonacceptance, the eternal story that I and the world need to be different than they are if I am to be happy. In the light of understanding what it means to extend unconditional friendliness to all things, we understand that aversion too asks to be befriended; it also is suffering that can only end through our willingness to be intimate with the landscape of ill will, so it can be understood.

The Buddha put it simply: "Hatred does not cease by hatred. By kindness alone is hatred healed. This is an eternal law."[3]

We become aware of the ways in which aversion shapes perception. When our mind is gripped by ill will, we perceive the world to be populated by imperfect people determined to unsettle, threaten, and harm us. Aversion creates isolation, mistrust, and defensiveness. When our heart is lost in ill will, we perceive only that which is broken and imperfect within ourselves. We can fear our own bodies, minds, and emotions in times of difficulty and devise strategies to dissociate from our own being. The narratives born of these perceptions turn back to deepen and reinforce the prevailing aversion, which in turn produces more narrative of judgment, fear, and blame. Ill will truly holds the power to make us ill as the body increasingly bears the brunt of aversive thoughts and emotions.

Metta, boundless friendliness, is intended to interrupt these harmful, closed feedback loops. Metta is a path of cultivation; we are learning to swim against the tide of habitual and impulsive habits and patterns that cause suffering and struggle. Metta is a behavioral gesture of the heart, as the Buddha put it: "What the mind reflects upon in a sustained way, to this our mind will bend and incline." We clearly recognize the harmful effects of ill will and commit to walking a different pathway. We sow the seed of intention in every moment of ill will: the intention to befriend and begin to see that our capacity to radically change our mind of the moment through metta is to change the shape of our world of the moment.

Metta is a present-moment recollection, a quality of mindfulness. If the inclination of mindfulness is to turn toward all experience, the inclination of metta is to learn that we can stand beside or near to that which we turn toward. We do not have to love the difficult, but we can care about it and befriend it. Each moment of befriending that which we have previously feared or abandoned makes a difference. The great power of mindfulness is that it enables us to choose what it is that we pay attention to and how we attend to all things. Metta and mindfulness, cojoined, are guardians of the heart. For the welfare and happiness of all beings, we embark on a journey of guarding our boundless heart. We learn that neither we nor the world can afford hatred. We discover the possibility of stepping out of the closed loops of ill will and learn we can stand near to all things and all moments without being overwhelmed.

When we read the Mettā-sutta, we may believe it is impossible for us to cultivate a boundless friendliness. Metta does not ask for the ambitious desire to save the entire world but simply to rescue the mind and heart of this moment from the compulsions of ill will. Metta asks us to be a guardian of all that we encounter in this moment—the events, experiences, and people who come into our world, to care for them all. Mindfulness and metta go hand in hand; both can only be cultivated in the moment we are present in; it is the only moment that can be transformed. We cannot have yesterday's or tomorrow's mindfulness or metta, just as we cannot have yesterday's or tomorrow's headache or loss. We learn to trust that each moment we make an attitudinal commitment to befriending rather than to aversion makes a difference. In each moment we commit our hearts to kindness, we are in that moment no longer consenting to feeding the habit of aversion, and we are thus bringing the tendency of ill will to an end. It does not imply that aversion will not arise again—it will. But its arising can be met once more with kindness and care. Each moment of cultivating the psychological gesture of kindness rather than the impulse of abandonment is learning to inhabit our life in a fearless way. In Shāntideva's teaching on compassion, he says, "The mind does not find peace, nor does it enjoy pleasure or joy, nor does it find rest or fortitude when the thorn of hatred dwells in the heart. Unruly beings are like space. There is not enough time to overcome them all. Overcoming these angry thoughts is like defeating all my enemies."[4]

There is an interwoven dynamic between ill will and metta, or boundless friendliness. Aversion is a destructive habit pattern and intention that invariably leads to suffering and unhappiness, stifling the heart's capacity for kindness. Metta is a wise intention and response that leads to happiness and the end of suffering. Within this dynamic, aversion is seen as the primary obstacle to kindness, yet kindness is the most direct and powerful way to dissolve and uproot aversion. Rather than meeting aversion with shame or condemnation, we learn it too can be befriended and understood. With the cultivation of kindness, we have a shift in perspective, no longer seeing aversion as an obstacle to be overcome, but the very ground in which metta grows.

If we listen closely to the moments of aversion and the moments of kindness in our days, there are two important aspects to notice. Aversion, whether in small ripples or larger waves is a generator of narrative—the intensity of the aversion tends to determine the length and intensity of the narrative that arises. We are prone to obsess about those we fear and dislike. Someone offends us—we feel our reaction and resistance arising and the beginning of the story about that person. Soon we have isolated every single thing that is unacceptable about that person. We may hardly even know the person, yet we weave enough narrative and conviction in the narrative through aversion to condemn him or her to being a lifelong enemy. It is also noticeable that the strength of the sense of "I," of "me," is determined by the strength of the aversion that arises and the solidity that is given to the "other." With the narrative grows the separation between "I" and "other." Distance and separation in turn become the breeding grounds of fear and the festering of ill will.

If we learn to listen closely to the moments of unhesitating kindness that can arise in our day, it also becomes clear that in those moments there is far less narrative. The sense of a centralized "I," or self, is almost imperceptible, and those moments leave no residues in the mind in terms of shame or judgment. In the moments of kindness we encounter, there is a quality of joy, a sense of relatedness, and a decreasing in the volume of both the sense of "I" and the sense of the "other." Kindness creates no enemies. It does not ask us to love every-one, but to learn to see through the eyes of respect and tolerance. Metta does not require narrative for its sustenance, but it is born of a heart rooted in courage and understanding. Metta is a practice of happiness and peace.

In developing our capacity for boundless friendliness, we learn to include the experience of aversion and ill will within that boundless-ness. Rather than feeling that aversion has to disappear in order for metta to arise, we learn to bring an attitude of kindness to the expe-rience of aversion itself, instead of making aversion into the "other" that we cannot accept. One teacher, Ajahn Sucitto, describes this as an affectionate curiosity. We begin to establish a dialogue and a relationship with aversion. What does aversion feel like? How do we sense it in the body? Can we stand next to it without flinching? How does aversion feel in the mind/heart? Is there a sense of agitation, tightness, or contractedness in the landscape of aversion? Can we stand next to that with our attention, explore and meet it with the gentle touch of kindness? We do not have to like ill will, but we need not feel bound to abandon it, and we can discover that it need not overwhelm or intimidate us.

The path of cultivating immeasurable kindness is a training of the heart and a commitment of intention. We have glimpsed moments of genuine kindness and friendliness in our lives; we know this is an inner capacity that like any other capacity can be developed and brought to maturity. The nature of immeasurable kindness is that it is not reserved only for those we love and who please us. It is perhaps not difficult for us to feel an unhesitating warmth and friendliness at the sight of a cuddly kitten or a smiling baby. It is far more challeng-ing for us to bring this same response to the person who insults us or intrudes upon our lives in an unwelcome way. Yet this is the invita-tion and the challenge of this path.

Metta is not primarily concerned with how we feel but with the attitudinal commitment and intention we bring to all moments of experience: to forsake the patterns of abandonment that aversion provokes, to learn we can stand next to all events and people and befriend them. Metta is a commitment of the heart: it swims against the tide of one of the prevailing ideologies of our time that tells us that how we feel about something is the ultimate authority that guides how we speak, act, and relate. The myth of authenticity asserts that if we feel good about something, like something, or are flattered by someone or something, it is worth pursuing, staying close to, investing in, and befriending. The myth that reifies feeling as an authentic guide in our moment-to-moment relationships equally asserts that if we don't feel good about something, dislike, or are threatened by someone or something, then it is only human and reasonable that we push it away, abandon, or ignore it and do our best to distance ourselves from it. Looking at our lives we see how many of our choices, strategies, and actions are guided by this myth—at times it is referred to as "being true to ourselves." If we investigate this pattern without judgment, we may instead discover we are "being true" to emotional habits that do not serve us well.

Both mindfulness and metta invite us to question this mythology, to begin to understand that, rather than representing authenticity, it may be describing a life in which we unconsciously and consciously agree to being governed by the predominant reaction, emotion, and mental state of the moment. Looking at the world around us we clearly see there is no shortage of beings who have equated emotional reactivity with freedom. Racist or abusive language becomes a right because it is part of our freedom. We can strike out at another in anger because we are free to do so. Neither metta nor mindfulness condemns the turbulence and power of our emotional and reactive inner world or suggests that we should suppress or ignore the impulses and emotional reactions that arise; the suggestion is to bring a gentle awareness into that world out of concern for the well-being of all beings. We learn to bring into the world of emotional turbulence a few simple questions: Does this lead to suffering or the end of suffering? Does this lead to a deeper sense of relatedness or to increasing alienation? Does this lead toward freedom or lead away from a liberated heart?

Immeasurable kindness is not so much concerned with how we

feel but how we relate to all feelings, people, events, and experiences. Kindness is only meaningful if it is embodied, the ground of our speech, acts, and choices. It is an expression of a profound concern for the end of suffering and the peace that is possible for all beings. It is returning again and again to the commitment and intention to abide in kindness and to befriend all moments of experience. It is learning to sustain that intention and to allow it to be the guide through the tangled and complex world of emotion, relationship, and action. We learn it is possible for genuine kindness to be the source of all our thoughts, words, and acts. It is an invitation to move from the world of habitual reactivity to a responsive life that treasures the well-being of all beings. We learn to honor the intention of kindness, and in that dedication it grows, deepens, and becomes the home we abide in.

A parent with a newborn child gets up in the night to tend to its needs; it may be the very last thing he or she feels like doing, yet a parent is guided by the commitment to care and not how he or she feels in that moment. A friend in distress reaches out to us for help—we drop our busyness and respond. It may not be how we feel, but our response is guided by a deeper sense of compassion. A frail and elderly person stumbles on the road in front us— unhesitatingly we offer a supportive hand without that act being filtered through the lens of how we feel in that moment. People on a meditative pathway will find themselves in many moments finding their way to their meditation cushion or seat even though they might in that moment feel that it would be much easier to follow an avenue of distraction or avoidance. These are all acts of embodying a deeper commitment to aspirations and intentions, rather than following the predominant mind state or feeling of the moment.

The pathway of metta has mindfulness woven into it. It is a path that asks us to remember the intentions that heal and liberate in all moments of forgetfulness. The path of liberation and transformation found in the brahma viharas is as concerned with what we do and how we live as much as it is concerned with inner development. We do not have to feel generous in order to live with generosity; we do not always have to feel compassionate in order to respond with compassion. Liking or loving something is not a prerequisite to befriending all things and to having kindness be the abiding place we commit to. Just as our minds have an impact upon our actions, so too do our actions have an impact on the shape of our mind and heart.

A student recounted how she committed herself for a year to have her speech rooted in metta, to use words of kindness and gentleness rooted in empathy and respect. She said there were many moments she was tempted to fall into harsh speech, condemning or judging or just engaging in social gossip. She said each morning she renewed the commitment. It did not mean that the aversive, harsh thoughts didn't arise, but in their arising they were met with mindfulness and kindness and rarely made their way into her speech. She said it was a practice that changed her life. She found that people trusted her, turned to her in their most difficult moments without the fear of being judged, that her friendships deepened and her difficult relationships began to ease.

We set our feet and our lives upon a path that draws on the enduring and transforming aspirations and intentions that have the power to heal and liberate our hearts and our world. In every moment of our lives, whether silent or speaking, still or moving, we are always practicing and enacting something. It may be habitual and unconscious; it may be responsive and intentional. This path of awakening invites us to know this, and awareness teaches us that in every moment there is a choice about where we make our home. Where we make our home—whether in the world of fear and aversion or the home of kindness, mindfulness, and befriending—will inevitably shape our thoughts, words, and acts and how we perceive the world. It is a challenge for us to learn to liberate the moment, to liberate our hearts from fear and aversion. It is also the path to a life of joy and freedom.

In her poem "Kindness," Naomi Shihab Nye writes that it is only in seeing the size of the cloth of sorrow that we come to understand that it is only kindness that makes sense anymore. Hand in hand, mindfulness and metta ask us to open our eyes and hearts to the sorrow of our world, to be touched by the struggle, fear, and violence that damage and scar the lives of so many. We are asked to truly sense the helplessness of those trapped in poverty, neglect, and deprivation, to open our eyes and hearts to the threads of despair, loneliness, and pain that leave too many people in our world forgotten and invisible. Then it is true that only kindness makes sense anymore. To commit ourselves to kindness in our thoughts, words, and acts and to be a conscious participant in healing the world we are part of. Metta brings us out of the shell of self-absorption, allowing us to be touched by the world and to touch the world with kindness. With friendliness and kindness we take our place in the family of all beings.

In one of the early texts, the Buddha describes this, saying:

Looking after oneself, one looks after others.
Looking after others, one looks after oneself.
How does one look after others whilst looking after oneself?
By practicing mindfulness, developing it and making it grow.
How does one look after oneself by looking after others?
By patience, non-harming, friendliness and caring.[5]

Metta teaches us that one cannot pursue peace, happiness, tenderness, safety, and freedom only for oneself. My peace, happiness, and freedom is linked to and interwoven with yours. My confusion, fear, and sorrow is also linked to and interwoven with yours. Metta teaches us to move from the language of "I" and "you" and into the language of "us" and "we." It is a universal language that honors the deepest longings of the human heart—to live with safety, to be protected, to be respected, and to be seen with kindness and respect. The universal language of metta knows that all of our thoughts, speech, and acts leave a footprint upon the world, and moment by moment we are learning to touch the world of the moment with kindness.

The Path of Metta

The conscious cultivation of metta as a meditative pathway employs the use of a few simple phrases that give shape and language to the intention of metta. There is nothing sacred about the phrases that

I will suggest. It is important to find words that are meaningful to us, that we can use with ease. The words are secondary; they are the ways that we begin to learn to sustain the intentions of kindness and befriending. Traditionally the way we have inherited the metta practice is to invite into the field of our attention the various domains of human relationship. We turn our attention to ourselves, to someone we regard as a benefactor, to a good friend, to someone we are more indifferent toward, to a difficult person, and finally expanding to all beings, known and unknown.

This style of practicing metta is a skillful means; the method is the way that we begin to make our home within the intention to befriend and to cultivate an attitude of kindness. As an insight practice we would use the phrases slowly, allowing space between the silent articulating of each phrase—as if listening to the silence between the calls of an owl in the night. With each phrase we are planting the seeds of intention in the ground of mindful stillness and then listening inwardly to whatever response arises. There is no right response; we are not trying to contrive a particular feeling or state of experience. There may be a whole range of different responses: impatience, boredom, agitation, or aversion. There might be responses of warmth, of tenderness and brightness—all are welcome and included in the intentions of befriending that are planted. Rather than expecting we should feel some loving glow, we remember that the practice is concerned with learning to sustain the intention of befriending and allowing it to plant its roots in our hearts.

There is a psychological and emotional process involved in the cultivation of metta. We begin by remembering, bringing to mind a person and relationship where there is an ease of befriending available to us. An aspect of the Pali word *sati*, usually translated as "mindfulness," is this quality of remembering or recollecting. In the cultivation of metta we are remembering our capacity for boundless kindness. Not only are we establishing a present-moment recollection, but we are remembering our deepest values and intentions and our capacity to embody those intentions. We remember a recent encounter with a person or an event that has had an unmistakable taste of metta, unhesitating kindness. There is a trackable psychological process involved in the cultivation of metta as we learn to incline the heart toward befriending. The recollection of this past event is brought into the present; we attend to it with mindfulness, and it becomes a present-moment recollection. Through sustaining our attention within the felt sense of befriending, we learn to deepen and sustain the capacity of our hearts to abide in kindness. As we learn to incline our hearts toward befriending rather than toward aversion and abandonment, on the subtlest level, new neural pathways are being laid. On a psychological and emotional level, metta, as a way of being present, becomes increasingly naturalized.

· THE PRACTICE ·

BEGIN BY FINDING A PLACE where you can sit in a comfortable position and establish a posture of calm alertness. Allow yourself to settle into the posture, feeling all of the places where your body contacts the cushion, chair, and ground, bringing awareness to the sensations that are present. Sense the sounds and the stillness around you. Allow the thoughts of past and future simply to sit in the background of your attention, and begin to establish a present-moment recollection. Include in that mindfulness an awareness of your present-moment mood, the climate of your mind/heart: a simple noticing without judgment or ideas about the mood we think should be present.

As much as you are able to, invite into the field of your awareness a recent encounter with a person or event where there was an unhesitating sense of friendliness, of warmth, appreciation, or generosity, remembering an encounter that has gladdened your mind and brought a smile to your heart. It does not need to be a particularly dramatic or special memory—the smile of a child, an unexpected gesture of kindness from a stranger, a meeting with someone you care about. Allow that person to sit in the center of your attention and listen inwardly to whatever response arises in the present with that remembering. You are simply sensing the felt sense of gladness associated with the image. As you hold that person in your attention with kindness, begin to offer your well-wishing for his or her well-being.

> **May you be safe and well.**
> **May you be peaceful.**
> **May you live with ease and with kindness.**

Allow the phrases simply to rest in your awareness. They are not invocations or commands, but simple offerings of generosity and kindness. Some students like to simplify and use only one simple phrase or even just one word. Let there be space between the phrases, and in those spaces listen inwardly to whatever response arises as the phrases are silently articulated. When your attention drifts away or becomes hijacked by streams of thought, just gently return your attention to the intentions of befriending and mindfulness by gently returning to the phrases.

> **May you be safe and well.**
> **May you be peaceful.**
> **May you live with ease and kindness.**

In the cultivation of metta, we begin with the domains where there is the greatest accessibility to our own potential for kindness and friendliness. We develop the felt sense of what it means to establish our self within those intentions before bringing those intentions to more emotionally complex areas of our experience. We are learning to be intimate with the landscape of unhesitating friendliness. This is a practice that is not confined to a meditation cushion with our eyes closed. This is a practice for our lives. Every moment is an opportunity to cultivate kindness. On hold on the telephone, waiting for a bus, standing in line in the supermarket may be moments we dismiss with frustration or impatience, but they are fertile moments for consciously cultivating our capacity for befriending the present just as it is.

As we go out into our lives and the myriad of encounters each day brings, we learn to keep the intention of befriending close to our hearts. It can be deeply helpful to begin to notice the small and large moments in our day when we offer and receive unhesitating kindness from those we know and those we don't know. We can learn to acknowledge and honor those moments intentionally, offering a simple, silent appreciation and well-wishing.

May you be safe and well.
May you be peaceful.
May you live with ease and with kindness.

Befriending Oneself

The Buddha was very clear in stating that we could search the entire world and not find anyone more deserving of kindness and care than ourselves. In traditional teachings of metta, the cultivation of unconditional and immeasurable kindness toward ourselves is placed at the beginning of the path. For many people this is the most challenging, complex, and difficult domain of the practice. At a meeting with Western teachers some years ago, the Dalai Lama expressed astonishment in learning of the levels of self-judgment and self-hatred Western students directed toward themselves. We live in a culture of a centralized self where perfection is demanded. It is a culture of individualism, where the ongoing demand to prove ourselves, to succeed, and to strive to earn love and to be worthy of happiness and acceptance are central tenets. It is a culture with a built-in failure mechanism. Subscribing to this culture is to subscribe to the ever-present sense of never feeling we are quite good enough, forever falling short of our self-imposed standards of perfection. The language of this culture is laced with aversion—the background symphony of self-judgment, inwardly directed disparagement, and contempt. The mechanism of this culture of the perfect self manifests as well-practiced pathways of self-abandonment, self-harm, and disdain.

Depression is epidemic in our world, scarring and limiting the lives of millions. There is some initial research that suggests that the cultivation of metta in the landscape of depression can be a trigger for further rumination and relapse as it highlights the degree of estrangement that may be a reality in our lives. The cultivation of metta within these deeply embedded psychological and emotional patterns of self-abandonment needs to be undertaken with great care and sensitivity. It remains a truth that there is no one in the world more worthy of care and kindness than ourselves. The most profound shift any of us can make as a human being is the shift from aversion to kindness, from abandoning to befriending. It is a shift from creating and re-creating patterns of suffering and anguish to cultivating and reculti-vating patterns of well-being and peace. It is perhaps unrealistic to anticipate that we will find peace and kindness inwardly if they cannot be found within our own hearts.

It is important to remind ourselves that metta is not a state or an emotion separate and apart from more difficult or afflictive states and emotions. It is an attitudinal commitment and way of being cultivated within all states, particularly in the midst of aversion and patterns of abandonment. Metta teaches us a way of being present with all states, all emotions, with an attitude of befriending. The tendency of aversion is to separate ourselves from the afflictive and imagine a way of being in some future moment, where affliction has ended, allowing some more idealized state of kindness to emerge. To see metta as an idealized state separate and apart from the sorrow and sadness of the moment would inevitably be a trigger for a renewed surge of feelings of failure and inadequacy. The pathway of metta is a present-moment recollection, befriending our sadness and sorrow, our judgmental thoughts, our feelings of failure and unworthiness— these too are suffering and are deserving of kindness. It is a rotation of consciousness; we are no longer waiting for affliction to disappear so that kindness can then emerge. It is through cultivating our capacity for befriending adversity that affliction will be eased and healed. With metta we learn to liberate the moment from the torturous grip of ill will and to make befriending our home.

· THE PRACTICE ·

ONCE MORE SETTLE your body into a posture of embodied ease and attentiveness, and begin to cultivate a present-moment recollection. Be mindful of your body touching the ground, the sensation of your hands touching your legs. Sense the sounds arising and passing; cultivate a receptive awareness. Sense what it is to inhabit your body and this present moment with an affectionate curiosity.

Bring your attention to the life of your body, with the spectrum of sensations that are present in this moment. Sense the places in your body where there is tension, holding, or discomfort. Touch those places with a gentle, curious awareness—mindful of the subtle changes occurring within areas of discomfort, the ebb and flow of intensity, the changing nature of sensation. With mindfulness explore the edges of discomfort, where the solidity of pain turns into something else that is less contracted. Sense what it is to stand next to or nearby the difficult with mindfulness and care.

Listen to the life of your body, also sensing the places in your body that are at ease—the palms of your hands, the touch of your lips together, your ears. With mindfulness, stand next to all that is well, free from pain and distress. In this landscape of sensation—the well and the difficult, the easeful and the challenging—begin to plant the seeds of kindness and befriending. In this practice, the intention of metta as a relational intention is a process and is a verb rather than a noun or state. We are on a journey of befriending, caring, listening, and attending. We are in a process of relearning what it is to incline the heart toward kindness.

> **May I be safe and well in the midst of this.**
> **May I be peaceful within this body.**
> **May I rest with ease and kindness in this moment.**

It is not easy for us to stand close to the painful and the difficult. We may be aware of the deeply embedded patterns of aversion and abandonment arising. We don't want to be close to pain; we don't want to experience pain—this is human. We are, in the cultivation of metta, not asked to like or love pain or distress. We respect the very human wish for pain to come to an end. We also know we are often not in control of the uninvited experiences of illness and pain that will touch all of our lives. We hear the voice of self-judgment arising: "What did I do to deserve this?" "Pain is my fault." We learn we have choices about what we feed in any moment. If we feed the voices of judgment and blame with attention, thought, and reactivity, they will grow and strengthen. If we feed the intention of metta through returning our attention to the phrases of and the commitment to caring, that intention will also grow and strengthen.

If you find that your tolerance for standing near the painful begins to falter, you can experiment with bringing your mindfulness to the areas of your body that are well—absorbing a felt sense of ease. Pain is not the totality of your experience in that moment. Pain can coexist with ease and wellness. A significant aspect of boundless friendliness is in experientially knowing the possibility of peaceful coexistence between pain and wellness, the difficult and the lovely. We learn not to be governed by one aspect of our experience, the predominant impression of pain or distress, but to widen our awareness to embrace the whole of our momentary experience. If the voices of harshness amplify, you can return to the first practice—remembering and bringing into the present the recollection of a moment or encounter of unhesitating kindness. When there is a sense of being once more established within that intention, return again to the body, with its life of both unease and ease.

In Buddhist psychology there is a singular word in Pali (the language of the early texts), *citta,* denotes both "mind" and "heart." These are not seen to be separate domains of experience but are held jointly beneath the term *citta,* or "consciousness." *Citta* describes the world of psychological and emotional experience and their interaction with one another, which shapes our world of the moment. Our world of the moment is unique to each of us, although the way that world is patterned is universal in human consciousness. Our world of the moment is shaped by our emotions, the lovely and the afflictive; by our thoughts, the helpful, reflective, and creative thoughts and the unhelpful, obsessive, ruminative, and habitual thoughts. Our world of the moment is shaped by states of mind, sadness, spaciousness, contractedness, stillness, agitation, and calm.

In learning to be mindful of our own mind/heart, we begin to see that it is a changing experience, existing in a state of potentiality and being shaped moment to moment by thought, mood, and emotion. There is much in life that can afflict and challenge us, much that is sorrowful and conflicted. Yet there is little that afflicts us as deeply as our own mind/heart when it is shaped by habitual, confused, and reactive patterns that create and re-create struggle and anguish inwardly and outwardly. In the cultivation of metta, we are learning to befriend the mind/heart, to shape the mind/heart with kindness, and to liberate our heart from the ill will that causes so much distress. We are cultivating a mind/heart that is a true friend, a refuge, capable of deep creativity and understanding where we can abide.

· THE PRACTICE ·

ONCE MORE FIND a posture of ease and alertness, and establish the mindful intention to be present, to inhabit the body and this moment wholeheartedly. Sense the places of stillness and calm within your body—the stillness of your hands, the quietude of your posture, the stillness around you—and bring an awareness of that stillness to the forefront of your attention, allowing the passing thoughts and images to sit in the background of your attention. For a few moments simply trace the movement of your breathing from its beginning to its end, with each out-breath releasing any sense of busyness or agitation.

Widen the field of your awareness to include your entire body, sensing the calmness embodied in your posture and the aliveness of sensation within your body. Befriend the entirety of your somatic, embodied experience, without reservation or preference. We are prone to be disembodied beings, living in our thoughts and leaning forward into the next moment, attending to the body only when distress demands it of us. Both mindfulness and metta ask us to dissolve the separation between mind and body. We begin to sense the interwoven process of body/mind. The body of sadness, the body of ease, the body of aversion, and the body of kindness come to be known in the light of a caring mindfulness. The Buddha proposed that everything there is to learn in this life will be learned within the length of this body. It is both the kindergarten and the graduate school of mindfulness and immeasurable kindness.

Widen the field of your attention further to sense the life of your mind/heart in this moment. Notice whatever mood is present— sadness, ease, anxiety, calm, dullness, agitation, or spaciousness— simply sensing the climate of the mind in this moment without any judgment. Notice too the range of thoughts and images passing through the mind—past, future, planning, obsessing, rehearsing, or worrying. As the thoughts arise, also allow them to pass like weather systems moving through consciousness. Sense what it is to stand near to all of this with an attitude of kindness, befriending the mind of the moment. Once more plant the seeds of intention in the midst of all of this.

> **May I be safe and well in the midst of all things.**
> **May I be peaceful in the midst of all moments.**
> **May I abide in ease and in kindness**

There may be many moments when you find your attention caught by the passing contents of the mind/heart. These are moments not to judge or despair but once more to renew the intention and to reestablish one's home in those intentions, articulated in the phrases. Mindfulness allows us to make choices in where we abide and dwell; metta teaches us a way of abiding free of ill will, permeated with kindness.

A Benefactor

Metta is a multispectrum word that embraces the many wholesome and ennobling qualities of kindness. One of these is the quality of generosity. Generosity is the foundation upon which the entire path of awakening rests. It gladdens and enriches our hearts and lives and the lives of all. It is the antidote to the fearful, defended heart that lives in fear of loss and deprivation. The threads of fear run through the whole of the fabric of aversion, leading us to cling ever more tightly to all that we call our own. The grasping mind, defined by fear, separates us from the family of beings and from the joy of generosity.

Generosity is no stranger to any of us. Our lives have been touched by unexpected small and large gestures of generosity offered to us by people close to us and by strangers. We know in our own experience moments of unhesitating generosity where we reach out to touch the life of another with an appreciative and responsive heart, and they are moments of gladness. Generosity is a responsiveness of immediacy that offers what this moment, this person, needs, unfiltered by our judgments of whether another deserves or is worthy of that response.

Traditionally, different aspects of generosity are described. Material, practical giving responds to the needs of another and alleviates distress—the generosity of caring for the well-being and happiness of another. There is the generosity of patience and our attention—our willingness to see and to listen to another wholeheartedly. The generosity of fearlessness reaches out to protect another from harm; it is generosity that allows us to be a true friend to another in all circumstances. In the Buddha's path of awakening, ethics rests upon generosity; a heart of stillness is rooted in kindness. Generosity is an embodiment of the deep understanding that there is truly nothing that we can call our own, and it is generosity that counters the forces of greed that lead us to see the world as a servant of the misguided belief in insufficiency. The generous heart is also presented as a path of cultivation, a quality we train and develop. We learn, as with all aspects of metta, to incline our hearts toward generosity in all moments, rather than toward withholding and defensiveness.

Generosity is not only an antidote to fear but to its close cousin greed, the ever hungry heart that can never receive enough, have enough, or be satiated. With metta we come to understand that fear and greed are experiences of profound suffering, not to be condemned or judged but to be befriended and understood. They are deeply embedded emotional habit patterns; they can be dissolved with generosity.

In the cultivation of metta it is the figure and the domain of the benefactor that embodies the quality of generosity. In moments of loneliness and disconnection, our lives can feel bereft of benefactors. Too many people have grown up in families and environments scarred by harshness, rejection, and coldness, where there has been an absence of benefactors. Yet none of us would be here today, breathing, living, and endeavoring to walk a path of awakening, without our lives being touched by many acts of generosity, support, inspiration, and kindness. In moments of desolation and loneliness, we may struggle to find anyone who we feel is a true benefactor. These are the moments we feel most separated, apart, and unsupported. Yet as we bring a gentle kindness and investigation into those moments, we can begin to see the ways in which our lives and our stories are intrinsically interwoven with the lives and stories of all humanity. The food we eat, the clothes we wear, whatever safety we have—all have come to us through the efforts of many people we will never meet. As Martin Luther King Jr. wrote, "Before we even walk out of our door in the morning we are already indebted to half of the world."

In reflecting upon the benefactor in metta practice, we are not asked to recall someone who has dramatically rescued us from a burning building or heroically stood between ourselves and danger. Our benefactors may be people we have never met but who have inspired us from afar with their courage, selflessness, and commitment—the people we admire for who they are and for the wholesome changes in our world forged through their dedication. Our benefactors are those who have supported and cared for us through their words, acts, and care. They are the people who comfort us in moments of distress, who guide us when we feel most lost, who encourage us when we feel most despairing, and who have confidence in our capacity in our moments of darkest doubt. Our benefactors are the many people we say thank you to on a daily basis as they ease our way through the world with simple acts and words of care and kindness.

As we introduce the domain of the benefactor into our practice, we may also reflect on the ways that we are a benefactor, not only to others, but also to ourselves. Are there ways in which we offer the priceless gifts of generosity, patience, and confidence to ourselves? Can we learn to be a benefactor to ourselves, offering compassion, forgiveness, and tolerance to our own body/mind experience? Can we learn to see through the veneer of our own imperfections and faults to honor the seeds of great stillness, understanding, and compassion that lie within us? Can we learn to be generous inwardly with our attention, honoring our capacities for steadfastness and courage?

· THE PRACTICE ·

TAKING ONE'S SEAT in a posture of ease and alertness, once more begin the practice by bringing a caring, sensitive attention to the life of your body, the felt sense of aliveness in all of the sensations presenting themselves to your awareness. Sense the life of your mind/heart—mindful of the process of thoughts and images arising and passing, holding on to none. Cultivate a sense of ease, a present-moment awareness.

Invite into that space a memory of someone you regard as a benefactor—someone present in your life now or from your recent past. Recollect that encounter; if you can, visualize that person and let him or her sit in the center of your awareness, or simply rest in the remembering of the person you appreciate. As you do this, simply sense whatever response arises inwardly—any glimmer of thankfulness, appreciation, gratitude, or happiness. With mindfulness, sense the imprint of those qualities in your body and mind. As much as you are able, sustain your attentiveness with the image or recollection of that person and offer to that person your heartfelt wishes for his or her well-being and happiness. Allow plenty of space between the articulated intentions, sensing what it is to dwell in that well-wishing.

May you be safe and well.
May you be peaceful.
May you live with ease and kindness.

After some time explore what it is to bring that same generosity and appreciation to yourself and your own experience. Sense what it is to be a benefactor to yourself—generous with your respect, your care, and your kindness.

May I be safe and well.
May I be peaceful.
May I live with ease and kindness.

It may be helpful to alternate your attentional focus between the person who you feel the most unhesitating appreciation for and yourself. Explore what it is to abide in thankfulness, in gratitude, and in kindness. In the cultivation of metta, it is important to keep the practice free of striving and forcing, free of the expectation that something should happen or some specific emotion should arise. Metta practice is always a simple invitation and a conscious cultivation of intention and inclining our hearts toward kindness.

A Friend

Friendship occupies a pivotal role in the Buddha's path of liberation—it is one of the three pillars of awakening. As much as the Buddha taught the blessings of solitude and aloneness, he chose to live his life in community and venerated wise community as the very ground for learning to awaken together. Understanding the nature of friendship is a key to understanding the immeasurable quality of metta. In the cultivation of metta, friendship is turned into a verb— learning what it is to actively, intentionally, and consciously befriend all people, including ourselves, all events, and all experience. As it says in the metta discourse:

With friendliness for the whole world should one
Cultivate a boundless heart
Above, below and all around
Without obstruction, without hate and without ill will.[6]

None of us walks this path alone; we rely upon trusted and noble friends. One of the greatest challenges in our lives is to be a trusted and noble friend to ourselves and to others. Our friends are as fallible as we are; metta knows how to forgive imperfection and to embrace fallibility. Friends sustain and comfort us in moments of desolation, friends gladden our hearts, and friends are a refuge in times we feel we have no refuge.

Human relationships are the most tender and vulnerable places in our lives, rife with the potential for great heartache and great happiness. Friendship asks of us great effort and great honesty if these relationships are to deepen and be sustained. We are by nature relational beings—touching and being touched by the world around us. Within these relationships we are asked to understand what it means to be alone—a refuge to ourselves—and we are asked to learn what it means to be together, with kindness as the guiding intention in all our relationships.

The Buddha spoke at length about the nature of noble and trusted friendship, saying:

Trusted friends are those who are committed to helping and
    supporting us.
Trusted friends are steadfast in both difficult and happy times.
A good friend reminds us what is beneficial to us and is
    empathic.
Trusted friends protect us when we are forgetful and lost.
They are a refuge when we are afraid and are generous.
Noble friends guard your confidences and attend in times of
    misfortune.
A trusted friend steers you away from wrongdoing and is a
    companion on the path to awakening.

A good friend feels no need to flatter you or profit from you.
A trusted friend does not stray from the path of kindness.
The Buddha taught: Just as the dawn is the forerunner of the
     arising of the sun, so true friendship is the forerunner of the
     arising of the ennobling eightfold path of awakening.[7]

These are powerful guidelines that invite our reflection. Our lives
would be radically changed if we could learn to embody these guidelines in our relationships not only with others but with ourselves.
They offer us a way to understand how the foundations of trust and
honesty underlie friendship. They are guidelines that embody not
only genuine care and respect but also courage.

Cultivating metta, we cultivate an inner commitment to be a
trusted friend to ourselves and others. We reflect on the meaning of
friendship and the ways it is embodied in our thoughts, words, and
acts. Metta is not governed by preferences—responsive to those we
like and dismissive of those we dislike. It is learning to befriend the
world and to forsake ill will and enmity within. It is not a romantic
commitment that imagines ill will never will arise. In this world of
unruly beings, there is plenty of scope for ill will, mistrust, and fear to
arise. Metta teaches us to be wise within those surges—not to regard
them as signs of failure but equally to befriend the difficult.

As an attitudinal commitment, boundless friendliness holds
within it the intention to live in a way in which we hold no one as
an enemy, an opponent. Difficult people are part of all of our lives—
metta suggests we have a choice about how we respond to those difficult people. We can follow the pathway of judgment, disdain, avoidance, and abandonment, or we can learn to be still in the face of the
difficult, to stand near to those we are prone to cast out of our hearts
and lives. Difficult people may remain intractably difficult even if we
find the capacity to relinquish the fear and ill will we hold, but we
can be certain nothing can change in our relationships or in our own
hearts if we hold on to that aversion.

The cultivation of metta equally invites us to learn what it means to be a friend to ourselves, to befriend all aspects of our experience in body and mind, to protect ourselves and remind ourselves of what is beneficial in the pathways we follow in our minds, to be generous with ourselves, forsaking the harmful patterns of self-directed ill will and enmity. Metta teaches us a way to be steadfast within the moments of happiness and unhappiness we experience, knowing there is no greater gift than the gift of kindness.

· THE PRACTICE ·

ESTABLISH A POSTURE of alert and gentle attentiveness, being mindful of the present-moment experience of your body. At times it is useful to spend some minutes attending to your breathing process, inhabiting both your body and the present moment fully. Attend to cultivating a kindly attentiveness free of striving or forcing. If it is helpful, once more remember a moment in your day where there has been a glimpse of appreciation, generosity, or well-being. The foundation of metta practice is a sense of ease and the willingness to be present, free of expectation and demand.

Invite into that space a recollection of someone you regard as a friend, present in your life now or from your past. If you can, visualize that person or simply recollect your last encounter with the person. Recollect a person who brings a smile to your heart, a sense of appreciation and happiness. As you engage in this, simply listen inwardly to whatever response arises. If the memory or image brings with that the associated sense of gladness, explore what it is to allow that gladness to pervade your body and mind. Remember it is not an invitation to recall nostalgic stories or become lost in the emotion but a way of reminding ourselves of the intentions and inclinations that underlie friendship. Begin to offer the friend living in your attention your heartfelt wishes for his or her well-being.

> **May you be safe and well.**
> **May you be peaceful.**
> **May you live with ease and with kindness.**

After some minutes bring your attention back to yourself, exploring what it is to hold yourself in those same intentions. Include whatever pains or discomforts that may be present in the body, whatever unwelcome thoughts that may appear—befriending all. Offer to yourself those same simple intentions for your well-being and peace. Once more in the midst of difficult sensations or experience, cultivate the willingness to befriend the body just as it is.

> **May I be safe and well in the midst of this.**
> **May I be peaceful in the midst of this.**
> **May I live with ease and with kindness in the midst of this.**

The cultivation of befriending and being a friend to all who come into our world is not a practice reserved for a meditation cushion—it is a practice for our life. Many people come into our world each day—those we care for and those we flinch from with fear or irritation. In all of those encounters, we explore what it means to abide in kindness—to be steadfast in the lovely and the unlovely with a mind unbounded. There is a courageous commitment in the cultivation of immeasurable friendliness—to abandon no one, to turn toward all people and events with a heart unshaken.

Equally it is helpful in our day to be mindful of all the moments we are not a friend to ourselves: the moments of judgment and blame, the moments we neglect our well-being, and all the moments we cease to listen to the messages of our own minds and bodies. These too are moments to pause, to renew the intentions to stand near to ourselves with kindness and care. Each moment we remember to do this, we interrupt habitual patterns of self-abandonment and learn to forge a relationship with ourselves that is rooted in friendliness.

The Neutral Person

The next domain of this path of cultivating immeasurable kindness is traditionally referred to as "the domain of the neutral person."[8] More accurately it may refer to the many people who pass through our lives that we feel indifferent toward. Between the poles of the people we feel affectionate toward, the people we love and care about, and the opposite pole of those we dislike, fear, and struggle with lies the much larger realm of people who barely register on our radar. They are the people who sit behind the supermarket cash register, stamp our ticket on the train, sit beside us on the bus, pass us on the street, or collect our garbage. We know them by their function; they make a fleeting impression on our consciousness but rarely do we see them fully as the living, hoping, feeling, struggling human being they are.

With the mindful cultivation of kindness, we open our hearts and our eyes to all beings equally. We begin to sense how self-referential we are in our perceptions and relationships. We want to stay close to those who please, affirm, support, and flatter us. We want to distance ourselves from those who threaten, disturb, or challenge us. In many ways these are understandable human responses, yet the result is the exile of countless people from our awareness and our hearts. In a very real way the domain of the people we initially feel indifferent toward is the most generous and selfless domain of the path of metta. Cultivating metta with those we love, our bond and appreciation deepens. Cultivating metta with those we struggle with, we hope to find some alleviation from the distress of that struggle. Cultivating metta with those we feel more indifferent toward is an act of profound generosity and care. They will likely never know they have been invited to sit in our hearts and attention; there is no profit in it for us. There is scope for considerable learning. Wise attention has the effect of making the invisible visible to us. Both metta and mindfulness have the effect of illuminating the moment we are in through the sincere attentiveness we bring to seeing and listening wholeheartedly. Mindfulness does not require drama and intensity. Mindfulness is deepened by our willingness to attend with care to the ordinary, the countless encounters with our world that we dismiss as being insignificant simply because they fail to excite us. In the light of mindfulness the world becomes alive, dynamic, and enlivening. In consciously attending to the people in our day we are indifferent to, they too are illuminated in the light of metta. Indifference disappears in any moment we see another person wholeheartedly.

We begin to sense the ways in which our relationships are primarily rooted in narrative and history. We share with our friends and loved ones past experiences, preferences, views, values, and opinions. Our stories intersect; we can revisit the past together and can imagine a future together. We may like the same books, support the same sports teams, and together our lives are defined by our mutual stories and history. We live both in a state of knowing one another and in a state of safety which rests upon familiarity. We find comfort in that familiarity and can be startled when people change in ways we did not foresee.

We also share with the difficult people in our lives a narrative and a history, often rooted in pain. Our relationship with them is defined by that pain. Even when we have done our utmost to remove difficult people from our lives, they live on in our thoughts, memories, and imprinted hurt. Someone who has hurt us in the past may disappear from our lives yet the injury remains. We may catch sight of such a person ten years later and feel the sense of injury arising and being relived. He or she remains the difficult person, frozen in the grip of our fear and hurt.

Our relationship with those we feel indifferent toward, the neutral people who pass through our lives, is characterized by the absence of history and narrative and thus the absence of emotional response. The outcome of this is to not truly to see them as being like us, beings who long for visibility, to be fully seen and accepted for who they are. Our attention is disinterested; they are a stranger to us, without personal meaning. The cultivation of metta interrupts and reverses this pattern. We learn to attend with care to the person before us and to see people fully. This domain of metta is an invitation to cross the boundaries of our personal story and the images and stories we hold about others and to explore the universal human story.

We do not need to know the details of a person's life for that person to be befriended. We learn to care rather than to neglect, to attend fully rather than to dismiss, and as we do so indifference vanishes. The universal human story speaks of the mystery, the hopes, and the complexity of every human being. We long for happiness and respect. We long for life, for relatedness, for love, and for acceptance. We long to be free from pain, struggle, and fear. Perhaps above all we long to be visible, to be seen, and to belong. This core longing is equally shared by the person who stands before us, not reliant upon any shared history or narrative. This domain of metta is primarily concerned with crossing the boundaries of "self" and "other" and to include all beings, without preference, in a boundless kindness. It is not concerned with the past or future of our relationship with the person before us but with the quality of our awareness and relationship in the present.

Indifference can be transformed into care through our intention to attend wholeheartedly to the person who stands in front of us. We cultivate a way of being in this world where no one needs to earn or be deserving of our care and no one is deprived or exiled from the boundless kindness possible for each of us. It is a present-moment attitudinal commitment to the well-being of another and the well-being of our own hearts, knowing they are interwoven.

This domain of metta practice is challenging simply because the people we feel indifferent toward are the people who are most forgettable. It can be helpful to begin to cultivate the practice in the midst of our everyday experience. Go into your day with the intention to bring a wholehearted attentiveness to those we may be more prone to ignore or overlook. Sense what it is to look into the eyes of or greet the conductor on the train, the person behind the counter at your corner shop. You are not asked to feel anything in particular, simply to see and to allow that person to be visible. As we do this in the day, we soon discover that indifference is sustained by inattentiveness.

The moment we attend, indifference disappears. The neutral person is no longer neutral. We may be tempted to begin to weave a narrative about him or her, but we can also restrain from that temptation and simply sustain a bond with that person that is rooted in the intention to befriend.

· THE PRACTICE ·

ONCE MORE FIND a quiet place to sit and settle your attention into the body, knowing that every moment of somatic awareness is a moment of mindfulness and present-moment recollection. Cultivate a sense of quietude within the body, breathing in, calming the body and mind, breathing out, calming the body and mind. Bring into your attention a recollection of a person or situation where kindness arises easily, sensing the landscape of ease, spaciousness, and friendliness.

Recall the intentions of metta:

> **May I be safe and well.**
> **May I be peaceful.**
> **May I live with ease and with kindness.**

Now invite into your attention someone neutral from your life, a person you have felt more or less indifferent toward but can recollect. If you can, visualize his or her face, or simply see him or her as you have seen the person—driving the bus, sitting behind the cash register, sitting beside you on the train, the neighbor you pass on the street but rarely acknowledge. Let that person sit in the center of your attention, in the center of kindness, and offer to the person your heartfelt wishes for his or her well-being.

> **May you be safe and well.**
> **May you be peaceful.**
> **May you live with ease and kindness.**

Your thoughts may wander; your attention may drift; stories may begin to form. We should not be surprised or discouraged. Simply come back to the intentions articulated in the phrases. Listen inwardly to whatever responses arise, leaving plenty of room between the phrases. From the focus on that one person, experiment with expanding the field of your awareness, bringing in more people who have in the past been invisible, shrouded with indifference, making room for them in that ever widening circle of kindness and friendliness.

The Difficult Person

People insult and betray us, offend and irritate us, and at times deeply harm us with their thoughts, words, and acts. We engage in heroic efforts and strategies to keep the difficult people in our lives at a distance, to avoid them, and to shut them out of our lives. Even when physically successful in doing this, they haunt our thoughts and our dreams as if we carry scar tissue from our encounters with the people we fear or feel harmed by. We have difficult people in our past, we will meet difficult people in the present, and it is likely we will all have our own measure of difficult people in our future.

It is the domain of human relationship where we most clearly perceive, feel, and at times are overwhelmed by aversion and anxiety. We do not want to experience and to repeat pain; this is human, and at times it is wise and skillful to know how to protect ourselves without turning that skillful discernment into a means of fueling fear and anxiety through thought and avoidance. An embodied kindness in our lives must necessarily also be a skillful kindness, which can be protective of our own well-being without being a fearful defensiveness. Metta engages with discernment, knowing how close we may stand to the difficult people in our lives. Metta practice within the domain of difficult people is not a magical solution that will transform difficult people into wonderful people. They may well stay difficult— we do not hold in our hands the capacity to change the patterns of another person's heart or mind just as another person does not hold the power to change the shape of our heart and mind. Cultivating metta in relationship to difficult people is not a condoning of the unacceptable and harmful. We will all be asked in our lives to find the courage to say no to the causes of suffering and find the skillful means in words and in actions to bring suffering to an end. The intention of metta without the next step of the embodiment of that intention in our interaction with life renders it meaningless. Metta allows us to act with courage to intervene skillfully whenever suffering is encountered.

The path of metta is concerned with the pain of living with a heart imprisoned by aversion, ill will, and fear. None of these afflictive emotions are a life sentence; with mindfulness we see that every moment of aversion is a moment of suffering deserving of care and compassion. We become preoccupied with the people we fear and dislike; they occupy our thoughts. We can find ourselves thinking more about the people we dislike or fear than the people we love. Through our preoccupations with the rejection or judgment we have received from another, we come to doubt ourselves; we can feel bound to the past experience of hurt, and in very real ways we can surrender our autonomy to the person who has hurt or harmed us. A person may have moved on in his or her life yet seem to have established residency in our hearts. The path of metta is concerned with healing this pain through uprooting aversion.

None of us will be exempt from receiving the aversion and harshness of others in this life. Words and acts of judgment, cruelty, and ill will, received from others, wound us deeply. It is all too easy to meet those expressions of aversion with our own aversion—ill will meets ill will, and ill will is compounded. Enemies are born, and each time we revisit the narrative of hurt, separation and fear are solidified. We can make our home in aversion rooted in pain, and it is a shabby and impoverished dwelling. Rumi, a Sufi master, once said, "Fear is the cheapest room in the house and I would like to see you in better accommodation." Metta suggests the genuine possibility of releasing ourselves, liberating our hearts from the prison of ill will, and finding that the keys are in our hand. The path of metta is concerned with liberating the heart, to know what it means to live and to die without enemies. The Buddha taught:

All that we are now is the result of all that we were.
All that we will be tomorrow will be the result of all that we are
    now.
There is a more contemporary adage—
If you want to know about your past, look at your mind now.
If you want to know about your future, look at your mind now.

We cannot rewrite the past with all of the experiences of hurt it holds, we cannot defend ourselves against the future with the experiences of difficulty it will bring, but we hold in our hands the capacity to transform the shape of our mind in the present. It is this inner capacity that the cultivation of metta is concerned with. Memories from the past arise in the present in the form of repetitive and often obsessive thinking. The associated emotional memories of hurt arise with the thoughts, and each time we dwell within them, those emotional memories become more deeply embedded and assume an almost addictive quality. We don't want to be endlessly ruminating on what has gone, nor have the past distort our present— too often we feel helpless in the entanglement with thoughts and memories.

These are the moments when it can be skillful to use the metta practice more as a concentration practice. The articulated phrases of the intentions of metta are thoughts. The human mind does not entertain two thoughts in the same moment. We have choices about the thoughts we sustain; it is far wiser and kinder to establish our attention in thoughts that are conducive to our well-being than in thoughts that inflict more harm upon us. In the moments when our mind feels gripped by aversive narrative, we can use the metta phrases in a more continuous and unbroken way. We may not feel kind, but we are not feeding the story of ill will. We can use the phrase "May I be safe and well in the midst of this. May I be peaceful." Or we can use just one phrase. It can even be helpful just to use a single word: "peaceful" or "kind." Learning to interrupt the pattern of aversion that relies upon thought that stokes the fires of ill will is a significant aspect of metta practice.

When the cascade of obsessive thinking calms, we can begin to explore the landscape of hurt and injury with a mindfulness imbued with kindness. In the teaching of the Buddha, liberating our hearts is likened to freeing ourselves of indebtedness. He invited us to reflect on the anxiety, worry, preoccupation, and emotional contractedness that are part of the experience of being financially in debt, to also imagine what it would be to repay the debt and the sense of freedom that would bring. In the path of liberation, the indebtedness that is spoken of is emotional and psychological indebtedness. If we want to know where this exists in our lives, we need only to be aware of what we most frequently dwell upon and obsess about. There is no power greater than aversion to create the pain of indebtedness. Dwelling in pain, shame, guilt, and ill will reveals to us all that we are not at peace with, inwardly and outwardly. Metta is a path of peacemaking. In the areas of indebtedness in our lives, we learn to ask ourselves: What would I need to let go of? What would I need to cultivate in order to find the freedom from the grip of aversion, from the grip of what has already gone by, and to heal the present?

The Buddha was asked by a student: "Why is it that your nuns and monks are so radiant?" He replied: "Because they do not dwell upon the past with all that has gone by, do not lean forward into the future with anticipation and expectation, and because they are not preoccupied or obsessed with anything in the present, this is why they are so radiant." We should not imagine that the nuns and monks the Buddha lived with were people who had lived lives untouched by adversity, enmity, or difficult people. Yet the Buddha's approach to healing was focused not so much on the story of what had gone by but on our relationship to that story as it emerged in the present. To bring ill will to memories of hurt is to bring the past into the present and solidify the sense of injury. To learn we can bring qualities of care, kindness, and metta to the reemergence of the past in the form of thoughts in the present is to learn we can heal the past through healing the present.

Metta practice begins with the places and relationships where there is the greatest ease of access to unhesitating kindness and care.

We can, with ease, stand near to our loved ones, friends, and benefactors. We learn to familiarize ourselves with the taste of kindness and friendliness. We learn it is an intentional capacity we can cultivate and learn to abide in. Within the domains of ease, we learn to incline our hearts toward befriending and we develop the skills and confidence that we bring to the more complex and difficult relationships in our lives.

The difficult person we engage with in metta practice can also be ourselves. We begin to sense the ways in which our relationship to our own body/mind experience is a microcosmic view of the patterns that flavor all of our relationships. Yet we can be more extreme and adept in directing ill will inwardly than anywhere else in our lives. We become, in ill will, masters of self-judgment, blame, criticism, and contempt and begin to understand the urgency of making peace with our own body/mind experience. Healing in Buddhist psychology is not primarily concerned with what has already gone by, but with our present-moment relationship to the emotional pain of the past as it arises in the present. Can sorrow, memories of rejection and harm, and anxiety rooted in the past be met not with aversion but with kindness? Learning to stand near to all things, to befriend them with kindness, is the essence of metta.

In beginning to explore this domain of metta practice, it is not helpful to choose as the focus of our attention the most difficult person in our lives. It is skillful to bring into the focus of your attention a person whose recollection triggers only a murmur of ill will or irritation rather than an onslaught of narrative. We begin with what is possible rather than the impossible.

· THE PRACTICE ·

TAKE YOUR SEAT in a comfortable posture, allowing the body to relax and to settle. Cultivate an inner listening to the life of your body and your mind. Sense the thoughts and sensations arising and passing with a mindful kindness. Bring into your attention a person in your life with whom kindness and friendliness arises without effort.

Reflect on that person and your own response, cultivating metta as an attitudinal commitment.

> **May you be safe and well.**
> **May you be peaceful.**
> **May you live with ease and with kindness.**

Turn that same attitude of kindness toward yourself—your body, mind/heart—however you are in this moment, whatever you are experiencing in this moment. Embrace your own being with the same unstinting kindness you would offer to a loved one.

> **May I be safe and well.**
> **May I be peaceful.**
> **May I live with ease and with kindness.**

Allow space between the phrases, and listen inwardly to whatever response arises. Allow your attention to expand to include the friend, the benefactor, the neutral person, and yourself, and once more make your home within the attitude of befriending.

> **May we be safe and well.**
> **May we be peaceful.**
> **May we live with ease and with kindness.**

Extending your attention further, invite into the field of your awareness someone you do not feel at peace with. You can almost imagine the person sitting on the cushion next to you or in the next room. Once more visualize that person, or recall your last encounter with the person. Listen inwardly to your own response, however it is, and explore what it is to stand near to that person and your own responses to the person. Let the phrases be the anchor of your attention, rather than the historical narrative. As much as you are able, offer your willingness to befriend.

> **May you be safe and well.**
> **May you be peaceful.**
> **May you live with ease and with kindness.**

If you find that ill will or anxiety arises and intensifies, explore what it is to also find a refuge inwardly in the midst of those difficult emotions.

> **May I be safe and well in the midst of this.**
> **May I be peaceful in the midst of this.**
> **May I live with ease and with kindness in the midst of this.**

If the practice becomes forced, it is always possible to return to a domain where there is more ease, to recover our capacity for befriending and then move once more to the difficult person. The cultivation of metta is fluid and responsive; it is learning to dwell within kindness in the midst of all relationships—freeing our heart of the moment from ill will and fear.

The World of Events and Experience

Traditionally metta is cultivated within the realm of human relationship, yet aversion is not reserved solely for our relationships with other people but is a familiar visitor in the world of many of the vexing and difficult events and experiences we encounter each day. For metta to be meaningful, it equally needs to expand to embrace that world. As a path of awakening dedicated to uprooting the toxicity and suffering of ill will, metta is cultivated in every moment that aversion arises. We learn again and again, with mindfulness and clear intention, that we have choices about where we make our home—in the contracted home of aversion and fear or in the spacious home of metta. As the poet Ikkyū writes:

My real dwelling
Has no pillars
And no roof either
So rain cannot soak it
And wind cannot blow it down.

We will all experience in this life our own measure of loss and disappointment. Unwelcome change comes to us; there may be moments when all certainty is stripped away and our worlds crumble. Unexpected pain and illness come; people we love suffer; jobs are lost and plans overturned; we are separated from people we care for. There are the great hardships and grievous losses that will be part of our lives, and there are the innumerable moments of disappointment when life is just not how we want it to be. Trains are late, computers freeze, the car breaks down, and our colleagues fail to support us.

We live in a conflicted world where we are exposed on a daily basis to the reality of the cruelty, violence, prejudice, and deprivation that human beings experience and are capable of inflicting upon one another. Metta is not a means of dissociating from this world but an invitation to find a way to live within it, free of ill will and harshness. It is a commitment of the heart to the possibility of living in this complex and challenging life without fear and without adding fuel to the fires of ill will.

How do we respond to this troubled world we cannot control? We feel the tremors of fear and anxiety, the familiar patterns of resistance and turning away. At times we may seek to find refuge in numbness or feel our hearts harden in blame. This is what we do with the underlying feeling of helplessness in the face of the difficult, not knowing another way to respond. Metta is a training in nonabandonment. We are not asked to love or even like the difficult, but we learn the profound strength, courage, and spaciousness of metta, which rescues the heart from being overwhelmed not only by the difficult but our own reactions to the difficult.

As it is said in the metta discourse:

Let no one despise anyone anywhere;
Let no one through anger or hatred
Wish for others to suffer.
As a mother would risk her own life
To protect her child, her only child,
So for all beings one should
Guard one's boundless heart.[9]

Learning to protect our own heart, we learn to protect the world. Learning to protect the world of the moment, we are learning to protect our own heart. We learn to protect our heart and the world from the injury of ill will. Restraint may be part of this wise protection. Restraint is not avoidance or suppression but caring for what is being fed in any moment of our lives. Aversion and fear arise; their future is determined by the quality of attention we bring to their arising. The primary fuel that guarantees a future for aversion is thought. This is where we learn to practice restraint, learning it is possible not to enter the gateways of judgment, blame, shame, and contempt. Restraining our thoughts is the forerunner of restraining words and acts of harshness and aversion. We learn what it means to protect the world of the moment. Every moment of fear and aversion holds the potential to be a turning point that rests upon learning to guard our boundless heart and thus guard the world.

We can learn with mindfulness to know thoughts as they arise and also to allow them to pass. We learn in the moments of fear and aversion to renew the intention to stay close to the moment, however difficult it may be. We can with mindfulness bring our attention to our body of the moment, establishing a dialogue with the somatic sense of fear and aversion. In the midst of events and experience that lead us to feel threatened or overwhelmed by fear and aversion, we can find refuge in the more formal metta phrases. Metta is not a one-dimensional cultivation using only the phrases. Aversion and fear are somatic and affective experiences, shaping our mind and body of the moment. We can learn to stay close to those experiences and imprints, exploring them with mindfulness, softening rather than hardening, opening and embracing rather than closing, and learning it is possible to begin to befriend all events and experiences.

Cultivating a benevolent heart, a mind of friendliness with the world of events and experiences is clearly a training for our lives, a present-moment cultivation in all of our encounters with life. Metta is an intention we take into our day, into our relationships, our work, and all the ways that we interface with the world. It is more than just a formal articulation of the phrases. It is a careful examination of all the moments and places we avoid because aversion or fear has been reified. It means being mindful of our speech, knowing its power to harm or to heal. Metta invites us to pause in the midst of the difficult events and experiences of our lives and to ask: What does this moment need? What does it mean to care for this moment, this person, this experience we find ourselves in? Metta is always relational, a way of being present within our life; it is engaged and dynamic. We ask of ourselves the core question: What is needed to liberate this moment from ill will and fear and abide within a boundless heart?

· THE PRACTICE ·

THE FORMAL PRACTICE can be a great refuge and companion brought into all the moments we are prone to abandon. With mindfulness we reverse this pattern that solidifies aversion and turn toward the moment rather than flee from it. With the intention to befriend, we bring the willingness to stand as near as we are able to the difficult or challenging experience of the moment or even to the small moments of irritation and vexation. Metta in this moment is a verb and a process, an intentional inclining of the heart.

> **May I be safe and protected in the midst of this.**
> **May I be peaceful in the midst of this.**
> **May I live with ease and kindness in the midst of this.**

The Boundless Heart

There is a core altruism to the cultivation of metta, a core benevolence and care, free of preferences and partiality. All beings are worthy of metta; all beings benefit from metta—it describes the most liberated and caring way of being in a world that cries out for the generosity, mindfulness, and kindness that metta brings. As beings training on a path of awakening, we are asked to sensitize ourselves inwardly, to let the integrity of metta be the foundation of all our thoughts, words, and acts. For the ennobling qualities of the heart to emerge, we are asked to be intimate with all people, events, experiences, and ourselves. We cannot befriend from a distance; compassion and joy are not born of dissociation but of intimacy. We learn to open our eyes and hearts, to see and respond with care to everyone and everything that come into our life without exclusion. We discover that it is possible to change the course of our minds, to free them from ill will and to make our home in goodwill. This is a moment-to-moment cultivation, rooted in our daily experience with all it brings—the lovely and the unlovely. Life is the classroom of metta, the classroom where we explore what it is within us that leads us toward awakening and freedom and what leads to suffering and alienation. Committed to metta we become a conscious participant in healing our world. As the Buddha put it: "This is the most noble way of living in this world, here and now."

TWO

Compassion

ALTHOUGH THE WORLD IS FULL OF SUFFERING,
IT IS FULL ALSO OF THE OVERCOMING OF IT.
— Helen Keller

A young trainee neurologist found himself managing the case of young man, Paul, who suffered irreversible brain damage after being involved in a catastrophic cycling accident. Confined to a wheelchair, arms and legs moved by endless spasms, on a ventilator, no longer able to communicate, he sat with a tortured expression in his eyes— the only part of himself he had any control over. Humanity seemed to have disappeared, leaving behind only, it appeared, the primal emotion of rage. He growled, howled, and moaned—despite themselves the nursing staff found it difficult to be around him. The neurologist found himself doubting the commitment to sustaining Paul's life so artificially, wondering whether Paul shouldn't just be allowed to die rather than prolonging his distress. He clearly had no prospect of a better future and only an intolerable present.

One day he was present when the young man's sister came to visit, bringing with her Paul's pet dog, and witnessed a transformation he would not have thought possible. As the dog licked his hand and nestled against his legs, the rage ebbed, Paul's body calmed, and just for those few brief moments, he was a person, a brother, someone who was loved and mattered and could still feel a bond with his treasured pet. He could respond to love. It was a moment, the doctor said, "when I became acutely aware of how the failure of my own empathy had relegated this young man in my eyes to be someone outside of humanity. I saw only the pathology and not the human being, deserving of compassion."

At the heart of compassion is the invitation to turn toward suffering. Just as the longing for love, safety, and respect is a universal longing and story, so too is pain a universal and inescapable story. Suffering is part of the story of our body and of all bodies—illness, frailty, aging, and pain feature in every life. Suffering is part of the story of our hearts and of all hearts. In the anguished moments of loneliness, grief, and fear that can touch our lives, we are convinced that no one else has ever felt this way before. Yet there may be a moment when we find the courage to open our eyes and hearts and see that same pain mirrored in the eyes and lives of everyone around us. Our minds can be tormented by obsession, by guilt, shame, judgment, doubt, and confusion, and we write the story of a self that feels separate and apart from all other selves, unworthy and inadequate. We may also find just a moment to pause, to look around us, and to come to know that this pain too is part of the universal story, not unique to us alone but the potentiality of every human mind.

Take a moment of quietude, sitting on the train, walking down the street, and genuinely notice everyone around you. Do we see anyone who is exempt from uncertainty, loss, and disappointment? Do we see anyone who is exempt from aging and death? Is there anyone we can see who has been successful in building defenses powerful enough to offer protection from change, sorrow, and pain? This awareness is not meant to depress us or deny the many moments of joy, happiness, and delight that are part of our lives. It is meant to sober us and encourage us to reflect upon what truly matters in this one precious life we have to live.

Compassion asks us to take our seat in the center of the landscape of pain and distress. We could visualize ourselves sitting in the center of an ever expanding circle of beings—those we know and love, those we struggle with or fear, and the many beings we don't know. Turning outwardly to this world, we begin to sense the sorrows and challenges in every human life. To turn away from pain and suffering is to embed ourselves in a life of denial, avoidance, and agitation—a life disconnected from the universal story of all beings. To turn toward the reality of distress and pain is to open the door to the immeasurable compassion possible for each of us and to take our seat in the family of all beings. Compassion dignifies our life, widening the circle of our concern to include and to care for all. The Dalai Lama once said, "If you want to know what compassion is, look into the eyes of a mother as she cradles her sick and fevered child." Compassion has the power to bring harshness and cruelty to an end; compassion heals our hearts even when pain cannot be fixed; compassion is the root of forgiveness, patience, and tolerance. The seed of profound and immeasurable compassion lies in each of our hearts.

Shāntideva taught: "Just as I would unhesitatingly reach out to touch and heal the wound in my leg as part of this body, why would I not reach to touch and heal the wound in another as part of this body?" Compassion is no stranger to any of us. In some of the most anguished moments of our lives, we may know what it is to receive the compassionate, tender touch and presence of another, when our hearts are softened by their care. Unhesitating moments of compassion are part of our emotional landscape—the moments when we reach out to another to help, to support, and to care. These can feel like fragile moments, arising only to disappear once more in self-absorption and busyness. Even as we treasure the uncontrived moments of compassion we all experience, they are easily forgotten in the momentum of our lives. The path of awakening teaches us not to leave these moments to chance or regard them as welcome but also accidental encounters. A genuine path of awakening treasures the well-being and safety of all beings and the embodiment of that intention in our thoughts, words, and acts.

Moments of unhesitating compassion—whether offered or received—leave a deep imprint on our hearts. They give us a glimpse into a world that is not defined by "I" and "you," "self," and "other," but a world where all living beings are joined in the longing to be free from harm, to be well, and to be cared for. The Buddha speaks of the possibility of immeasurable compassion, dedicated to the end of all suffering, and equally speaks of compassion as a path of cultivation. It is the primary aspiration of a spiritual life. The path of understanding and liberation taught by not only the Buddha, but by all great teachers, is not concerned with personal improvement or gain but with teaching us how to care. We do not step foot on our path of inquiry and cultivation with a compassion that is immeasurable, but with the seeds of compassion in our hearts that ask to be cultivated, tended, and brought to fruition.

Compassion is not a state or an emotion but an understanding. It is an understanding rooted in the classroom of our lives and hearts and in a genuine and honest investigation of our own relationship to pain and to suffering. This is the core, liberating insight in the cultivation of compassion. It is an invitation to go beyond the confines of our "self" story marked by our personal preoccupations, anxieties, and sorrows and to see the story of ourselves in all stories and lives. This is not to dismiss, diminish, or neglect the sorrows, the grief, and the fears that are very personal and real in our life. There are many moments of hurt and injury in our lives, and every moment of pain is worthy of all of the kindness and compassion we can muster. Yet that pain is more readily healed and cared for when it is not compounded by isolation and contractedness. Pain is pain, suffering is suffering, struggle is struggle—it is mine and it is ours. Compassion is as essential to our well-being and freedom as sustenance is to our bodies.

In the early teaching life of the Buddha, he summed up his teaching, saying, "I teach only one thing. There is dukkha and there is the end of dukkha." The entire path of awakening is dedicated to bringing *dukkha* to an end. *Dukkha*, a Pali word, is a compound word vital to understand if we are to understand compassion. It is a multidimensional word that speaks to the heart of human disquiet, dissatisfaction, and distress. The first aspect of this word refers to what is called "the pain of pain." The broken leg hurts; grief hurts; aging introduces us to a world of frailty that hurts; illness is not imaginary. We will all die. It is no one's fault—to live in a body is an open doorway to all the pain that can afflict a body. The pain of pain ranges from the minor discomforts our body experiences on a daily basis to chronic illness and a severity of pain that can feel unbearable. Life continues to teach us the lessons of loss and to find an inner poise and grace within the landscape of loss. Youth, vitality, psychological acuity, energy, and physical ability all diminish. We can mourn their loss with grace and wisdom but without despair or the belief that we alone should be exempt from pain. Our willingness to turn toward the realities and difficulties of aging, sickness, and death is the beginning of learning to live a life guided by compassion rather than by denial and fear.

The second dimension of this word refers to the essential instability of a world composed of conditions and processes that we cannot control. The sunny day turns to rain, and rain turns to sun. We can lose everything we count on for security and certainty. People come into and leave our lives. The delightful mood turns to a mood of sadness. Gain and loss, praise and blame, happiness and sadness all change— the world will not stand still for us. At times we welcome change; at times we mourn and resist it. The threads of impermanence are woven into every aspect of life—our bodies, minds, emotions, our possessions, our status, our opinions, the lives of those whom we love, and the lives of those whom we struggle with. Change is woven into everything we see, feel, touch, and experience and into the lives of those we love and those we disdain. It is neither positive nor negative, good nor bad—it simply is.

Every moment of experience is a matrix of process and conditions. Particular conditions come together, and we have health; others combine together, and we have illness. This interface of conditions and process shapes famine and abundance, deprivation and affluence. We are the children of all of the conditions that have preceded us: our parents, our environment, our culture—all come together to shape who we are and our life in this moment. All conditions—everything we have, the ground we stand upon—are ever shifting and ungraspable. It is a simple truth; there are no exemptions. We may be the most mindful, insightful person in the world, and our lives will continue to be inextricably interwoven with change and instability. It is not optional; it is not emotionally neutral; it is often sad. It is also not intrinsically suffering.

Understanding these first two domains of dukkha is central in the path of compassion. Loss, instability, aging, pain, and death merit compassion; the harsh realities of changing and uncertain life are softened through compassion. The unavoidable and inescapable changes that touch and alter our lives ask to be met with both understanding and compassion. Too often they are regarded as a problem, a failure, a trigger for agitated action. In many early spiritual traditions people sought ways to transcend this life and all its afflictions through self-mortification and denial. Our contemporary forms of denial take the form of self-judgment, numbness, and avoidance. A genuine path of awakening calls for transcendence, not transcendence of life but transcendence of struggle and anguish through understanding.

It is the third dimension of dukkha that the path of awakening and compassion is primarily concerned with understanding and caring for. It is the world of reactivity, born of confusion, that sets us on a road of perpetual argument with the first two domains of dukkha. The simile of the two darts is a poignant description of this domain of dukkha. Imagine a person being shot by a dart. It hurts; it would be equally painful for the most awakened being and the least mindful person in the world. How we respond to that first injury is the deciding element in whether we suffer or know how to bring suffering to an end. If that initial injury is reacted to with confusion, bewailing our fate, looking for who to blame, refusing to remove the dart until we know who shot it and why, a world of anguish and suffering would be constructed in that moment. It is as if we have been shot with two darts—the first the initial injury, the second injury being the world of despair, anguish, and aversion born of our reactions to the pain of the dart. With our reactions of aversion, fear, shame, and contempt, we pattern and shape our world of the moment. Our mind, heart, and relationship to life are patterned by habitual and repetitive reactions. The second dart is the source of the greatest suffering; it can be understood and relinquished.

Pain hurts and can be met with tenderness, mindfulness, and compassion. Change and instability disturb us and may be deeply sorrowful. This too can be met with a deep understanding of life's undeniable rhythms. Life can be challenging and difficult, but there is little that torments us so severely as feeling to be a prisoner of the reactions and fears that can govern our hearts. Learning to bring compassion to the world of our tumultuous and troubling emotional reactions is the beginning of releasing ourselves from the prisons of suffering that are created and re-created moment to moment through confusion and a chronic misalignment with life as it is: changing, at times painful, and always uncertain.

How we respond to the first dart is in our hands and born of understanding or confusion. Sudden loss and unwelcome change awaken us to the startling realization of how fragile our life is. None of our hopes, our dreams, our plans, or strategies can protect us from change and instability. It can be a terrifying or an awakening realization. It is possible that rather than traveling the habitual avenues of fear, aversion, and helplessness we can respond with insight and compassion. The habitual avenues of reactivity have the effect of disabling compassion and skillful action. Understanding dukkha deeply and profoundly, we are enabled to respond to our lives with the acts and responses that have the power to heal the moment.

Janet's much longed-for child was stillborn. She found herself descending into a spiral of depression that leached all joy from her life. She blamed herself, she blamed her husband, she blamed her doctors—she blamed the world. She lived in a landscape of loss and grief; she functioned but hardly lived. She described the point, a brief moment, when she glimpsed the ways in which she was creating and re-creating suffering and despair for herself with her blame and harshness. It was a moment, she said, of understanding that the pain of loss would be part of her life but perhaps did not need to govern her life. She described beginning to find the ways to be a littler gentler with herself and those around her, to begin to feel it was OK to be delighted even a little by the sound of the birds, to be able to smile at a baby with its mother without being catapulted back into the rawness of her own loss. She discovered, she said, what compassion might truly mean in healing her heart and that she could find the source of that compassion within herself.

I have come to feel that the shape of each person's life and sense of self are defined by their relationship to pain and suffering. If we fear suffering and pain, we will engage in a life of perpetual agitation dedicated to devising strategies to avoid pain. We will become busy, fixated on finding the solutions to fix the immediate pain in our life. We do not want to be in pain (understandable and human), yet in the denial of the pain and suffering that touches our lives, we can become masters of avoidance and dissociation, dedicated to annihilating pain and making it go away. Fearing pain we may choose the avenues of numbness—through drugs, alcohol, or simply through keeping ourselves busy and distracted. Stillness we perceive as endangering our defenses—if we are still, we may begin to feel not only our own pain but the pain of the world. We may choose to harden our hearts, not wanting to know about the famine destroying the lives of thousands, the wars claiming the lives of the innocent. Openness and connection feel dangerous when our hearts are bereft of inner resources; we are afraid of our own helplessness and incapacity to meet pain without being overwhelmed. Despair is one of our primary responses to the vastness of pain that can scar a human life.

None of these avenues of avoidance merit judgment or blame; they too are expressions of suffering and confusion, worthy of care and compassion. In the light of mindfulness, we come simply to understand that these familiar mechanisms of avoidance do not bring pain to an end but serve only to compound suffering. Mindful inwardly we become acutely aware of the numerous second darts that arise in our minds and learn we do not need to be lost within them. They may be habits of reaction and fear that have a long history, yet compassion begins with our willingness to meet and transform these habits and to learn to walk new pathways of responsiveness in the present. We learn we can turn toward rather than away from, to include rather than to exclude, to attend rather than to ignore, and to open our hearts to the cries of our own hearts and the cries of the world.

Compassion has a family of origin. Compassion looks backward to mindfulness and to the cultivation of boundless friendliness. Mindfulness inclines toward, turns toward, our present moment experience, reversing the pattern of aversion; the world is illuminated through mindfulness, free of judgment and preference. Metta is learning to stand near to all moments, people, and experiences, befriending all that has been illuminated. Metta is a process of sensitizing ourselves to the world we live in with all its joy and sorrow. Compassion is concerned with our response to the sorrow and pain illuminated through mindfulness and befriended with metta.

In the early teachings, compassion has two primary interdependent elements. The first of these is described in Pali as *anukhampa*— it is the profound empathy, the trembling, quivering of the heart in the face of suffering or pain wherever it is met, inwardly or outwardly. One who develops this capacity for empathy is described as one who pulsates with compassion or one who can truly listen to the cries of the world. Empathy is the forerunner of the second aspect of compassion; the Pali word *karuna* describes the engaged dynamic of responsiveness, the translating of empathy and understanding into our thoughts, words, and acts. Karuna is concerned with embodiment, the courageous engagement with the small and large manifestations of pain and suffering we inevitably meet. It is a commitment to healing suffering when it can be healed, uprooting the causes of suffering when they can be uprooted, and being steadfastly present in the face of pain and sorrow that have no end.

Empathy

Here, the doctor Richard Selzer recounts the story of one of his patients.

> I stand by the bed where a young woman lies, her face postoperative, her mouth twisted in palsy, clownish. A tiny twig of the facial nerve, the one to the muscles of her mouth, has been severed. She will be thus from now on. As a surgeon, I had followed with religious fervour the curve of her flesh, I promise you that. Nevertheless, to remove the tumour in her cheek, I had to cut the little nerve.
>
> Her young husband is in the room. He stands on the opposite side of the bed, and together they seem to dwell in the evening lamplight, isolated from me, private. "Who are they," I ask myself, "he and this wry mouth who gaze and touch each other so generously?"
>
> The woman speaks: "Will my mouth always be like this?" she asks.

"Yes," I say. "It is because the nerve was cut."

She nods, is silent. But the young man smiles.

"I like it," he says. "It's kind of cute."

All at once I know who he is. I understand and I lower my gaze. One is not bold in an encounter with a god. Unmindful of my presence, he bends to kiss her crooked mouth, and I'm so close I can see how he twists his own lips to accommodate hers, to show her that their kiss still works. I remember that the gods appeared in ancient Greece as mortals, and I hold my breath and let the wonder in.[1]

Empathy rests upon understanding. We learn through the cultivation of mindfulness and insight that we do not need to be overwhelmed by the vastness of suffering nor by the immediacy of seemingly unbearable pain we meet in the moment. We are asked to make peace with the unarguable laws of all life—the pain of pain and the pain that can be triggered by change and the instability of the world of conditions. Many moments in each of our lives ask us to lay down our arguments with the unarguable. A young woman, diagnosed with a chronic illness, spoke of the moment when she could lay down that tension and resistance, saying, "The moment when I could stop saying, 'Why did this happen to me?' and instead say, 'Why would this not happen to me?,' the healing could begin."

Empathy equally rests upon the steady ground of inner stillness. We learn we can cultivate a mind and heart that is not gripped by agitation and reactivity. We learn to calm the turmoil of our thoughts and cultivate an inner quietude. We learn we can step back from the compelling impulses to fix pain and find solutions to make suffering go away. Empathy restrains the compulsions that can be threaded with an underlying aversion. We cease seeking for reassurances and hoping for a better future. We learn with mindfulness what it means to be present in the presence of all things. In stillness we discover receptivity, the capacity to listen wholeheartedly to the whispers and cries of pain and sorrow. Cultivating inner stillness is a journey for all of us, learning to calm the body and mind and establish a home within a calm receptivity brought to all moments in our life. In stillness we find the capacity to turn toward pain and sorrow, and for our hearts to tremble.

Empathy is caring; we look into the eyes of the homeless person and see beneath the appearance and the story, the pain of being lost and abandoned. A young man, living on the street, said, "The worst part of being homeless is not the deprivation; it is the fact that no one wants to look you in the eyes." We listen to the news, and we sense beneath the statistics of death and cruelty the harrowing reality of the misery that human beings can inflict upon one another. We learn to listen inwardly to our own thoughts of harshness, the pain in our bodies, the sorrow of our losses, and allow our hearts to tremble, embracing pain as pain, suffering as suffering. Empathy is not concerned with the narrative of pain, its history or its future. Empathy does not seek explanations nor judge the pain we see, experience, and feel. It is cultivating the heart that can tremble in the face of all suffering.

Empathy is strengthened by equanimity, sometimes defined as the willingness to be equally near all things. Learning to strip suffering of the layers of blame, shame, and rage, we learn to be like a willow tree that can bend beneath the fierce winds of life yet not be broken. We learn to turn toward rather than turn away from pain and discover an inner balance stronger than the winds of an uncontrollable and ungraspable life. Equanimity rescues compassion from pity, protects the sensitized heart, and knows how to stand with poise in the midst of all things. It is where we already are. Reb Anderson, a much loved American Zen master, wrote, "Buddhas do not live in the suburbs of suffering, they live downtown." Amid the change, uncertainty, and ungraspable nature of our lives, we learn what it is to dwell within a heart that cannot be broken.

Empathy is an act of generosity. We are generous with our time and primarily with our attention. We learn what it is to pause rather than be lost in busyness, to attend rather than pursue distractedness in moments of crisis. When a loved one in pain urgently requires our attention and care, we quickly learn to simplify and focus our lives to be able to offer what is needed. At times all that can be offered is our wholehearted, tender care and attention. It is an offering often more significant and healing than all the prescriptions and solutions in the world. Empathy, we learn, needs not to be triggered by crisis, but by a deeper awareness of the ever-present nature of anguish in the world and its call for healing. We learn to see and to listen wholeheartedly and to make room in our awareness and heart for the many people who come into our lives. We know in our own experience the difference between being seen and listened to wholeheartedly by another or being offered only a glancing attention. We commit to offering this wholehearted attentiveness to all who come into our lives. Empathy is an offering of the generosity of forgiveness rather than blame, of care rather than judgment, and of stillness rather than reactivity.

We learn to be generous with ourselves. There is an ancient Greek belief that suggests that only those who don't deserve their suffering are deserving of compassion. The contemporary enactment of this belief takes the form of the mountains of self-blame we heap upon ourselves for the suffering we experience. We tell ourselves the long stories of all we have done wrong, the mistakes we have made, our core inadequacy, as a way to explain the suffering that has beset us. We may have the capacity to be generous and forgiving of others, yet deeply withhold that same generosity in relationship to the struggles, sorrows, and confusion we experience in our own hearts. We are quick in adding the second darts of shame, self-criticism, and blame to the difficult emotions and thoughts we experience. We also learn this is optional, that shame and blame are suffering, as worthy of compassion as a wound in our body. We sense the possibility of developing the empathy to listen inwardly to the cries of our own hearts as suffering that is greatly eased through generosity, compassion, and care.

Empathy joins hands with stillness, equanimity, mindfulness, and insight in the landscape of compassion. Compassion has an extended family, and an important and necessary figure in that family is patience. Patience begins when we relinquish the demand for a better, different past and the hope for a better, idealized future. It is a way of meeting the present, this moment with all its challenges and its possibilities. It is patience that allows us to begin a dialogue and establish a relationship with the struggles of the moment, rather than inhabiting the imaginary world, born of fear and aversion, of a future and a life that begins when pain and sorrow go away. Patience is not despair or hopelessness—it is dynamic and alive and underpins compassionate response.

Milarepa, a much revered Tibetan teacher (1052–1135 C.E.) offers a teaching story. Living in a cave in the high mountains, he returned from gathering firewood to find his cave inhabited by a host of angry demons. He employed every strategy he could devise to make the demons depart. He reasoned with them, he offered them prayers, he threatened them, he tried to ignore them, and one by one the demons disappeared until only the fiercest demon remained. Having exhausted all his mechanisms to rid himself of the unwelcome visitor, Milarepa turned toward the demon, saying, "Please stay awhile; bring your friends; make yourself at home." Approaching the demon, Milarepa, in an act of surrender, placed his head in the mouth of the demon, and the demon, in the face of Milarepa's act of nonresistance, fled.

It's a happy ending that stories and experiences of pain do not always have. The demons do not always go away but take up residence in our lives and hearts. Compassion and patience ask us to consider and meet this alternative ending. Chronic illness and pain do not magically disappear in the face of compassion; difficult emotions and thought patterns can be so repetitive they feel woven into the very fabric of our being and we struggle in each moment of their arising. We may have people in our lives that are intractable in their reactions that create and re-create difficulty for us and themselves. Greed and hatred feel endemic in the world. Suffering, alienation, and pain feel bottomless. We cannot make it all go away; we cannot change the course of another person's heart and mind. We cannot make another person happy or well, and we cannot make even the people we care about the most into contented and peaceful beings. We can learn to meet the moment as it is; we can learn to be patient with all things. We are not in control of conditions, but we are not helpless. Patience is the willingness and capacity to be with all things, events, and people without being invested in a particular ending or outcome. We can take custody of our own way of meeting suffering and meeting life. Patience is the peacefulness and stillness of settling into what is right here, inhabiting our life with care, tenderness, and concern.

Embodiment

Empathy and embodiment together are the nature of compassion. Empathy teaches us to listen to and understand suffering and its causes. Embodiment is concerned with what we do with that understanding. Embodiment asks for courage. A compassionate life is a fearless life. It is courage that rescues compassion from being only a fine sentiment restricted to those who are helpless and innocent. It takes great courage to have compassion be the guiding principle of our thoughts, words, and acts. Courage is needed as mindfulness awakens us to the depth and apparent endlessness of suffering in the world. Remarkable courage is needed to stay close to the suffering that feels unbearable. It is courage that enables us to look pain in the eye without wavering. Compassion in its deepest sense is immeasurable. It embraces the most difficult people in our lives, the most brutal people in the world. Compassion is concerned with meeting suffering and uprooting the causes of suffering: the greed, hatred, and confusion that scars the lives and hearts of too many in this world.

Martin Luther King Jr. reflected on his death and the manner of his funeral, asking that whoever delivered the eulogy should not talk too long. He said, "Tell them not to mention that I have a Nobel Peace Prize or three or four hundred other awards. I'd like someone to mention that day that Martin Luther King Jr. tried to give his life serving others. I'd like for somebody to say that day that Martin Luther King Jr. tried to love somebody. Say that I was a drum major for justice, for peace and for righteousness. And all of the other shallow things will not matter. I just want to leave a committed life behind." We remember the young man facing down a tank in Tiananmen Square, the Indian peasants protesting the salt tax walking unarmed into the squads of

armed British soldiers, the young nurses serving in the Ebola treat-
ment centers, the nuns in Calcutta going into the dawn to collect the
abandoned children. Our hearts are moved in wonder in the face of
the heroism embodied by the people who have changed our world,
by their dedication to uprooting the causes of suffering. They do so
through their acts and their willingness to engage with suffering and
its causes. They were not born saints or heroes but found in themselves a courageous commitment to say no to the unacceptable.

The courage of compassion is not the domain only of the saintly.
An elderly man takes on the care of his much loved wife, lost in the
twilight world of Alzheimer's disease. Parents love and raise cher-
ished disabled children. The young man on the bus confronts the
passenger shouting racial abuse. Compassion recognizes the ways
in which untold suffering is generated and regenerated through
thoughts, words, and acts of ill will, fear, and confusion and does not
turn away. We may indeed feel fearful in the face of cruelty and harshness but know there is something more important than our fear.

A monk, imprisoned and abused for many years, recounted to the
Dalai Lama the story of those years of pain. The Dalai Lama asked
him, "Was there ever a moment when you felt your life was truly in
danger?" He replied, "The most dangerous moments were when I felt
myself beginning to lose compassion for my jailers."

The courage of compassion is not always dramatic or heroic but
manifests in many smaller moments and ways. We find ourselves in a
situation where collective ill will is expressed in gossip. It takes courage to embrace the risk of unpopularity and to challenge the status
quo. We help a struggling neighbor, reach out to a weeping child,
and speak to the person begging on the street. Courage is forged in
the fires of the difficult; confronting the causes of suffering may well
bring exposure to unpopularity, judgment, and blame, which is difficult to bear. It is far more difficult to bear the echoes of disappointment in our hearts born of turning away from a life where well-being
and the end of suffering hinge upon our willingness to turn toward it.

Compassion is always engaged with life, not some remote reflection confined to our meditation cushion. We are always embodying

and practicing something in our thoughts, words, and acts in every moment of our life. It takes courage to be aware of what it is that is being embodied—fear or courage, ill will or metta, generosity or withholding, patience or frustration. The question of whether our life is rooted in compassion or disconnection is a present-moment question and often an uncomfortable one. We may become acutely aware of dissonance—the gaps that exist between our deepest values, aspirations, and intentions and the kind of footprint we leave upon the world with our thoughts, words, and acts that splinter into consequences we cannot even see. Compassion asks us not to be discouraged or disheartened by moments of dissonance, these are the very moments we are invited to reestablish our home in those deepest aspirations and manifest them in the ways we engage with life. Courage asks for perseverance, the willingness to realign our lives moment to moment with a compassionate heart. We cultivate and renew those commitments to healing suffering and uprooting its causes both inwardly and outwardly.

One of the core and transforming insights at the heart of compassion is the profound understanding of the insubstantiality of the notions of "self" and "other." Without this understanding, compassion can waver, be restricted to those whom we feel are deserving and exclude the many beings in this world whom we feel to be unworthy of compassion. Embedded in the ideology of a fixed, independent self, we live in a world where we are separated and apart from the "other." It is this divide that is the breeding ground of fear, mistrust, aversion, and alienation. The dedication to uprooting the causes of suffering addresses this core cause of division, sorrow, and conflict. Experiment with taking a few moments to sit quietly and reflect on how you know yourself and who you believe yourself to be. Perhaps we begin to get a glimmer that our knowing of our self in any moment is shaped by what is identified with and clung to in the moment. It may be our body, our thoughts, our emotions, our opinions that are identified with, and out of this the narrative of "self" is born. This mosaic of experience is crowned with our name—this is who we believe ourselves to be. Identification creates a sense of ownership—

this is who I am, this belongs to me—and through identification we endeavor to create a fixed center in a world where nothing is fixed.

Some of our "self" narratives are momentary and fleeting—I'm happy, I'm sad, I'm hopeful, I'm depressed, I'm angry, I'm peaceful. Even though we have seen these changing faces of "self" a thousand times in a single day, we are still fooled. Identification creates a state of amnesia; we simply forget that this is the "self" of the moment, quite different from the "self" an hour or a day ago, and we are deceived into thinking this is my eternal "self," who I am and who I will always be. Identification by nature seizes upon a particular and mistakes it for being the whole, like seizing upon the crescent and mistaking it for being the whole of the moon. Identification is suffering; it alienates and disconnects; it is too often devoid of kindness and compassion. We don't want to be the person defined by imperfection, and we want to be the kind of person free of difficulty and pain, and life becomes a story of avoidance and pursuit.

At times our "self" narrative is historical, gaining greater authenticity through its repetitive retelling. Recently in a store I arrived at the cash register slightly behind a young woman approaching from the opposite direction. She hung back, and I invited her to go before me. She looked at me in astonishment, saying, "That's amazing." When I asked what was amazing, she answered, "I am the kind of person people always ignore and barge in front of." It is a powerful "self" story reinforced with belief and identification. It is a story that shapes our experience of life, our sense of possibility and impossibility. It holds the potential for suffering, isolation, and despair.

At other times our "self" story is the story that has been told to us by others. We are not invulnerable to the messages we receive from people in our lives. Our own story is imprinted and shaped by our early relationships and the thoughts and reactions we have received from others, willingly or unwillingly. If we have been told we are unworthy, unlovable, incompetent, or inadequate often enough, and do not possess the inner resources that allow us to question the truthfulness of that story, it is likely it will be absorbed, internalized, and become a truth, the story that we live. Listening inwardly to the story of "self" that arises moment to moment, we can begin to sense that we are no longer telling the story, but the narrative is telling us who we are.

The understanding that allows compassion to bloom is rooted in understanding the insubstantiality of our "self" narratives, which by nature will create the narrative of the "other." Through the eyes of identification, we perceive life in a self-referential way, defining the world and other people by what they mean to us. From the perspective of a fixed-self view, we are prone to impose upon all things our view of them. Someone is good because that person supports my view of self; another person is an enemy because that person disturbs the view I hold of my self. I pursue everything that bolsters my self view and avoid people, experiences, and events that threaten to undermine my self view. We begin to posit intrinsic values into people, objects, and events—seeing them as holding the power to make us happy or unhappy. Through identifying with views of myself and of all things and all people, I endeavor to create a world that is safe and predictable. Yet the very nature of life, its intrinsic change and instability, is constantly challenging all of our views.

A friend who lived on the edge of open countryside heard rumors of a planned building behind his house. Determined to protect his privacy, he planted a hedge that grew prolifically. Soon it was so tall it totally obstructed the views of the hills he so loved. He came to the startling realization that in his effort to shut the world out he had locked himself in. Defending our view of self and holding steadfastly to our views of others, our world becomes increasingly small and stultified.

Compassion and understanding arise simultaneously. They nourish and sustain each other. In a path of awakening, there is no endeavoring to annihilate the self, to improve the self, or to disdain it. There is the profound invitation to liberate our hearts from all fixed views of self. Listening inwardly we see that not only our bodies and minds are processes, so too is our sense of self. There is no central controller, no command center, no edifice that remains unchanging. Identification and clinging have the effect of turning processes into states and definitions, and of turning verbs into nouns. Releasing the tendency to cling and to identify with the changing processes and events of our bodies, hearts, and minds, we liberate ourselves to be the fluid, changing, responsive human beings we have the potential to be. The freedom from identification and fixed views does not result in chaos or dysfunction but in a present-moment stillness and awareness that is the root of compassion.

We come to see that the only thing that keeps anything fixed in place, static, and impossible is our view of it. This applies to each of us. We see we cannot be defined by the contents of our minds or experience, and endeavoring to do this self-definition is too often an act of harshness that imprisons us in our views of who we are. Instead of telling and retelling ourselves the story of limitation and failure held within our judgments and narratives, we learn to listen and to question. We hear the familiar inner voice of blame: "I am a failure, I am hopeless, I am not good enough." And we hear it not as a statement of fact but as a thought and learn to question the truth of that thought. We bring in the query, "Am I?" This is our starting point to liberate the view of the moment rather than falling into the abyss of belief. It is an act of compassion for ourselves.

One of the greatest gestures of compassion we can offer to another person is to liberate the person from our fixed views of who he or she is, enabling him or her to be the fluid, changing person he or she can be. William Blake wrote, "If the doors of perception were cleansed, the world would appear as it is—infinite." Any view creates finiteness and limitation. Compassion asks us to move from a place of knowing based upon views, fears, need, and anxiety to a place of not knowing. Not knowing is not a state of confusion but a way of being present in which we can wonder, question, and learn. We allow ourselves to be surprised by ourselves, by others, and by life. Our capacity to deepen and grow as a human being may well hinge on our willingness to be surprised.

We begin to sense the ways in which we are prone to seize upon the appearance, acts, and words of another and to impose upon the other a definition and view that condemns that person to an eternity dictated by our view. Compassion deeply rests upon being able to question and see beneath our narratives rather than clinging to them. The most difficult person we meet lives with his or her own measure of fear and anguish. The most destructive and brutal people in the world are born of conditions and imprints we can never know. This never means condoning or justifying brutality and cruelty. We are always asked to commit ourselves to bringing the causes of suffering to an end. Yet the immeasurable nature of compassion means that no one is abandoned.

Shmuel Goldman, a ninety-two-year-old, wrote:

I have a friend. A woman I already know many years. One day she is mad at me. From nowhere it comes. I have insulted her, she tells me. How? I don't know. Why don't I know. Because I don't know her.

She surprised me. That's good. That is how it should be. You cannot tell someone: I know you. People jump around. They are like a ball. Rubbery, they bounce. A ball cannot be long in one place. Rubbery, it must jump. So what do you do to keep a person from jumping? The same as with a ball. You take a pin and stick it in, make a little hole. It goes flat. When you tell someone: I know you—you put a little pin in.

So what should you do? Leave them be. Don't try to make them stand still for your convenience. You don't ever know them. Let people surprise you. This likewise you could do concerning yourself. All this I didn't read in any book. It is my own invention.

The Path

Compassion is a pathway of cultivation with the power to liberate our hearts from greed, ill will, and confusion. Compassion has the power to liberate the world of the moment from alienation and fear. We learn to incline our hearts toward compassion, cultivating our capacity for profound empathy and our willingness to embody our commitment to bring suffering and its causes to an end. It is a cultivation of the moment. Some of the formal traditional practices of compassion remind us that this central aspiration is the path of healing and awakening. As a practice for our lives, it is rigorous, calling for courage and commitment.

The Blameless

Opening our eyes and hearts we see so much pain, anguish, and suffering that is neither self-inflicted nor inflicted upon others—it is blameless. A child is diagnosed with a terminal illness; a refugee driven from home by war seeks safety in a land where there is no safety; a young person is mugged on the street; children with bellies swollen by malnutrition stare at us from our television screens; a young woman, a passenger in a car, suffers life-changing injuries in an accident; someone we love descends into the darkness of dementia.

Compassion begins here: we sense the trembling of our hearts, and we learn to stay present. As much as we would wish this pain to end, there may be no immediate solution. As much as we would wish for that person to be safe and protected, it is not within our power to dictate this. What can we offer in that moment? Our wholehearted presence, our willingness to stay near, to do all that we can do and know it is never enough. A man spoke of watching his son descend into the hell of heroin addiction. He did all that he could, yet he could not change the mind of his child. He spoke of going to an art gallery and seeing a painting of a mother standing on the bank of a river watching in horror as her baby is swept away by the current. In the painting the mother has no arms.

Human tragedy surrounds us, and we are asked to bear witness, to listen deeply, to know this could be us, and to tremble in the face of suffering. It makes no sense any longer to talk about your pain or my pain but to stand in the midst of pain and sorrow. This is an intention, countering our tendency to turn aside in the fear that we cannot bear this. All of life asks us to find the courage to bear the unbearable and to abandon no one. We need to find the simplest words to articulate this intention.

· THE PRACTICE ·

SITTING QUIETLY, with our bodies at ease we establish a present-moment attentiveness, rooted within our bodies. Bring to mind just one recollection of someone living in the midst of fear, loss, deprivation, or pain, and seat that person in the center of your awareness. Sense whatever response arises inwardly, letting go of the story of pain, being mindful of the simple truth of pain. Empathy is twofold, embracing the person we have invited into our hearts and our own responses of despair and concern. The words are secondary; primary is cultivating our capacity and intention for empathy and responsiveness.

> **May you find peace.**
> **May you be safe.**
> **May you be touched with kindness.**

It is important not to force the words, allowing space between them, knowing they are the gesture of commitment we bring to stand firmly in the midst of sorrow and struggle.

The Difficult

If compassion is to be truly immeasurable, we are asked to cultivate it in the places that feel the darkest and most impossible. We cannot fathom or explain the brutality, cruelty, and harshness that exist in our world. We cannot comprehend the inner hell of a person that is translated into compulsive acts of rage and harm. Explanations fail and human history is a record not only of human greatness but of human depravity. We act as if it is possible to bring suffering and its causes to an end even as we know it is not possible for us to change the course of another person's mind, nor to protect all beings from harm and danger. We bear witness to the greatest acts of genocide and hatred and the smaller acts of violence, prejudice, and ignorance that scar the lives of many. We commit ourselves to nonviolence and compassion in all our thoughts, words, and acts and do all we can to protect all beings.

One of the ancient teachings in the Buddhist tradition gives voice to this commitment:

> May I be the medicine and the physician for the sick.
> May I be an inexhaustible treasury for the destitute.
> May I become food and drink in times of famine.
> May I be a protector for those who have no protection, a guide for travellers, and a boat, a bridge and a ship for this who wish to cross over.
> May I be a lamp for those who seek light.[2]

It is a lofty aspiration, yet it is the aspiration at the heart of the path of compassion. The greatest weapon our enemies have is fear, and we learn we can be fearless and reclaim our freedom and our capacity for compassion in the face of the unacceptable. Marian Partington, in her book *If You Sit Very Still*, writes of the agonizing journey she went through from heartbreaking loss to working in restorative justice. Her twenty-one-year-old sister disappeared; her bones were found twenty years later buried in the cellar of a serial killer. She wrote, "I reflected on what we do with our unresolved pain. Not expressing the pain can lead to suicide. Acting it out leads to violence and brutality. Wishing it away, repression or denial leads to physical illness. The only creative way forward with so much pain is to inch toward forgiving." She describes forgiving as an ongoing process, not a state, reminding herself that "I'm doing this not just for myself but for my parents, my children, for the next generation" and also for her sister's killer. Every day, she says, she reminds herself of her commitment to compassion, embodied in one of the early vows in traditional compassion practices. "I vow to release all sentient beings from suffering."

· THE PRACTICE ·

SITTING QUIETLY, befriend the body and mind of this moment. Cultivate an inner calm and ease. Begin by bringing to mind the image of a person dealing with misfortune or pain who is blameless. Sense the trembling of the heart and the wish to reach out to heal. Bring to mind the articulation of that intention in the phrases that sit easily within you.

> **May you find healing.**
> **May you find peace.**

Gently widen the circle of your care and attention to include someone you fear or disdain. Sense what it is to allow the person to sit in your attention without fear. Many responses may arise; we learn to listen to them. Aversion is not wrong; it simply compounds pain. Offer to yourself your own wishes to be free from fear and aversion, to touch them with compassion.

> **May I find healing in the midst of this.**
> **May I find peace in the midst of this.**

Explore offering those same intentions to the difficult person. Make your home within those intentions, rather than within the narrative. Be free to experiment, being fluid with your attention— moving between the blameless person, yourself, and the difficult person. Invite into the circle of your care and attention a person you struggle with, judge, or condemn. Sense whatever responses arise within, yet as much as possible sustain your attention with the difficult person. Rest within that focus, mindful of not becoming lost in the world of thought and association. What can be offered in that connection that has been established? What can be let go of? They are important questions to ask of ourselves as we seek for a way out of a relationship defined by fear or ill will. Can our hearts tremble in the face of the pain that has been generated and the person who has generated that pain? Can we offer the slightest gesture of forgiveness and understanding?

> **May you find healing.**
> **May you be free from sorrow.**

The difficult people in our lives may be the hardest for us to care for. They may also be those who are in greatest need of healing.

Compassion for Oneself

We see so clearly that aversion and fear fractures our relationship with all things. These most familiar reactions to pain and distress sentence us to closed feedback loops of self-judgment, shame, and agitation that compound pain. Compassion is the beginning of healing—it is a much needed ongoing journey and cultivation in our lives. We learn to touch our own world of experience in a new way—not demanding that pain disappears but knowing it can be embraced in a caring heart. Every moment of distress in our bodies, minds, and lives asks for our response—we learn we can be a conscious participant in our own healing and freedom, not always from pain but within pain.

The sorrows and losses of our lives, the pain in our bodies, and the difficult, unwelcome thoughts and emotions are not signals of failure or imperfection. They remind us we are part of the human story, and we learn to ask ourselves "What does this need?" rather than "How do I get rid of it?" We learn we can, with mindfulness and kindness, discern the difference between the story of pain and the actuality of pain. The story is endless; the pain is immediate. The story has no answer; the pain can be responded to. We learn we can take the "I" out of the center of our experience of sorrow; we see how the sense of "self" begins to fade with the release of the narrative. In the light of mindfulness and compassion, suffering is seen and known as suffering. It is difficult, it is challenging, but it is approachable, and we learn we can step toward it rather than fear it. Healing does not mean that pain goes away but that it can be held with compassion rather than with aversion.

We learn it is possible to have compassion for our body with everything it can and will experience in this life. Contemplating our body, we contemplate the life of all bodies. It is not easy to be an embodied human being—we tend to flee from the body in times of illness.

Our bodies store memories of trauma, and our body is the primary building block of self-image. We learn we can be intimate with our body, establishing a relationship of compassion and care that is the foundation of our relationship with all things.

We learn what it means to have compassion for our minds and hearts; it is the first step in cultivating a mind that abides in compassion. Contemplating your mind is akin to standing on the corner of a busy street—we hope that butterflies and rainbows will visit; often we get exhaust fumes and noise. Thoughts and memories come unbidden; obsessions and preoccupations take hold of our attention; difficult emotions appear and reappear like uninvited guests. The Buddha once said, "Who is my enemy? My mind is my enemy. Who is my friend? My mind is my friend." With mindfulness we come to understand that it is not the thoughts or the memories that imprison us but the authority that is given to them. We learn we can be mindful of our mind, affectionately curious. With compassion we come to understand that our mind is asking for healing as much as any other dimension of life that is distressed or fevered.

· THE PRACTICE ·

SITTING QUIETLY WITH ONESELF, be mindful of the life of your body, mind, and heart of the moment. Sense what is well—the places in your body that are at ease, the sounds that are registering, perhaps just the movement of your breath. Welcome and appreciate all that is well.

Sense what may be difficult or painful in this moment, areas of your body that feel distressed, listening inwardly to the difficult thoughts or emotions that may be present—sadness, depression, anxiety, rumination. Notice how they may register in the body. Explore what it is to touch the painful and the sorrowful with compassion. Sense what it is to allow your heart to tremble yet not be broken in the face of your own distress—knowing pain as pain, sorrow as sorrow. Explore what it is to consciously plant the seeds of compassion in the center of pain.

May I find healing.
May I find peace in this moment.
May I rest in care and compassion.

The words are not important; they are not commands or pleas but a way of remembering the possibility of embracing our life as it is and touching our bodies and minds with compassion.

We widen the circle of compassion to include all those whom we love—each with his or her own measure of joy and sorrow. We open our eyes and hearts to all those we don't know. We do not need to know the story of another person, to know that like us each person longs for peace, for healing for the end of suffering. We explore what it is to bring a compassionate awareness into all the ways we interface with the world. We see suffering and we learn not to turn away. We do all that we can to help and to heal. We learn that our hearts can tremble in the face of pain and yet be courageous. There may be no end to suffering and sorrow in this world, but every moment of compassion makes a difference. Immeasurable compassion is embodied compassion, rooted in our intention to live a compassionate life.

———————

Moment to moment we learn to incline the heart toward compassion, planting the seed of that intention in every moment when sorrow, pain, and fear are encountered, inwardly and outwardly. We care and attend to that seed through investigation, the cultivation of stillness, mindfulness, and kindness. For any seed to grow, flourish, and bear fruit, it asks for nourishment and care. The possibility of profound and immeasurable compassion lies within us; compassion ennobles our lives and enables us to be a conscious participant in the healing of our world.

· THREE ·

Joy

IF WE KEEP A GREEN BOUGH ALIVE IN OUR HEARTS, THE
SINGING BIRD WILL COME.
—Chinese proverb

Joy, it seems, mostly comes unbidden. We cannot plan or contrive joy, yet it touches our lives. Joy gladdens our hearts; it eases the mind; it has the taste of delight and happiness. We may associate joy with the dramatically happy and intense moments in our lives: falling in love, the birth of a child, a reunion with a treasured friend, the glorious sunset. Yet joy can take us by surprise, born of the simplest of life experiences. Our attention is caught by the sparkle of the dewdrop on the grass, the infectious laughter of a child in the playground, the smile offered by a stranger, the image of a penguin waddling along the beach. We are suddenly awake, present in our life, and our hearts are gladdened. Joy, we might say, is the song of the awakened heart.

Joy has its roots in mindfulness, which sensitizes us to our world of the moment. Mindfulness brings intimacy with all things. With mindfulness we simply learn to make room for joy, learning to see, listen, and attend to all things with a spacious heart. Mindfulness and boundless friendliness foster intimacy—for us to be deeply touched by anything in this life requires intimacy. The longing for joy is a universal longing, at the root of many of the life quests we commit ourselves to. We look for joy in relationship, in meditation, in nature, and in play. Joy not only gladdens our hearts, it brings meaning and intimacy to the fabric of our lives. It is in moments of joy that we feel ourselves to be fully alive, vibrant, and appreciative human beings. As Joseph Campbell once put it, "What we are truly seeking for is the experience of feeling fully alive."

In the presence of joy, our depressions and sorrows fade and are held just a little more lightly. Our preoccupations and obsessions no longer take center stage; our anxieties and compulsions are, for even just a few brief moments, banished. There is a sense of inner freedom in joy, a genuine taste of wakefulness. We long to recapture those moments; they can feel like accidents, fortunate encounters that fade too quickly, only to become a memory we want to recapture. We can be relentless in the project of trying to regain the affective memory of joy—something wonderful is easily turned into an object of craving. In the path of awakening, joy, like kindness and compassion, is not left to chance. The seed of joy lives in each of our hearts; it is a capacity and a potential of the human mind. We learn to cultivate joy, to understand the roots of joy, to sense what it is within us that obstructs the arising of joy, and, with practice, to abide in joy in all circumstances of our lives.

In the teaching of the immeasurable and noble qualities of the heart that liberate us, joy is not referred to as a transient, episodic state but as a way of seeing, a way of being, and an embodiment of understanding available to all. In our emotional world, we polarize states—the welcome and the unwelcome, the desirable and undesirable, the worthy and the unworthy. The tendency to welcome and pursue the pleasant and to disdain and avoid the unpleasant and unwelcome is an understandable pursuit, but it is a recipe for a frustrated and agitated life. We believe that if sorrow and depression are present, joy must necessarily be absent. If joy is present, all unhappiness and anxiety will be forgotten. Cultivating joy as a way of being in the midst of all the conditions and events of our life is an invitation to radically transform our understanding of joy, experiencing it not as a state but as the place where our heart rests. We learn to cultivate the gladdened heart in the midst of life with all its difficulties and challenges.

A veteran grievously wounded in combat spoke of his life as a triple amputee, saying, "I cannot be grateful for what happened, but in truth I have never felt more alive than I do now. Despite the pain and the daily grind of making my life work I no longer take anything for granted. I have never treasured my children more. I learned to pause more and feel the life around me. I have become a better listener. Every day I am grateful for something."

Living for a time in a community of Tibetan refugees in India, I felt puzzled by their infectious joy, their laughter and apparent light-heartedness, their beaming smiles and generosity. Each of them had endured so much adversity and loss, witnessed cruelty and violence, and lived with an abiding awareness of the hardship being suffered by those left behind. Their lives as refugees were deprived and dire, yet somehow their hearts were intact and their joy embodied and shared with all who came into their world. Their profound generosity and kindness permeated their speech and actions and touched friends and strangers equally.

It is easy to romanticize the war veteran, to imagine the Tibetan refugee to be a saint, yet they would be the first to disclaim this. We meet people who live with a gentle joy in the midst of adversity, who are generous in the midst of personal hardship, who embody vitality and aliveness in the most challenging circumstances. Rather than idealizing these people, perhaps we can begin to ask ourselves where the roots of joy lie in ourselves. In the midst of our sorrows and losses, our challenges and pain, we ask ourselves whether we are truly dispossessed from joy or have simply forgotten the possibility of a gentle gladness in the midst of all things. We can perhaps remind ourselves of the capacity we have to make our home in a gladdened and contented heart. We do not have to wait for the difficult and challenging to end for joy to begin. Joy is not a denial of sorrow or an artificial contrivance but an inclination of our hearts that softens and eases the difficult. An early Chinese teaching of meditation invites us in the practice "to enter the gates of ease and joy."

In the teaching of the immeasurable and ennobling qualities of boundless friendliness, compassion, joy, and equanimity, joy is spoken of much less than the other liberating qualities of the heart, but it does not occupy a more lowly place. Joy brings serenity and kindness to equanimity, protecting it from coldness or remoteness. Joy is a necessary companion to compassion, softening the intensity and rawness of the inevitable pain we are asked to embrace. Joy motivates and inspires us to persevere in the face of seemingly immeasurable ignorance and suffering. Joy brings the inner spaciousness that protects the heart from being overwhelmed and is a refuge of contentment and ease we can learn to abide and rest within. Life brings affliction and adversity; we have no choice but to meet it. Our capacity to know a deep inner ease and gladness allows us to meet the difficult without rejection and fear. There are many, guided by compassion, who serve and care for others struggling with great difficulty and pain. The ongoing exposure to the pain in our world can deplete and exhaust the heart. Joy is the quality that restores and renews our intentions and capacity to serve. The phrase "compassion fatigue" indicates not the exhaustion of compassion but points to the depletion of inner resources, particularly spaciousness and gladness. Facing the world with so much affliction, it is crucial to remember to care for our own well-being and resource ourselves inwardly with joy and kindness. Gladness allows us to find rest even in the midst of action. Joy helps us to remember and to treasure our capacity for ease and peace.

In the traditional teachings of the boundless abodes, joy is primarily referred to as empathic, altruistic, or appreciative joy. It speaks of our capacity to celebrate, honor, and rejoice in the happiness and well-being of another. This is a significant aspect of the fabric of joy, tempering our tendencies to envy others, to compare ourselves to others in ways that we feel ourselves to be deprived or inadequate, and to come to know a selfless joy in the face of another's happiness. Yet for us to know this specific dimension of joy, it is essential for us to know the vastness of the landscape of joy.

Gladdening the Heart

There is much we receive from life that sparks joy. The simple delights of a good meal, a beautiful sunrise, time spent with loved ones gladden our hearts. Listening to a joyful piece of music, reading an uplifting poem, seeing a painting of great artistry can all be moments imbued with the taste of joy. They are moments that offer us a glimpse of our own potential for gladness, our heart's capacity to celebrate. In those moments we remember we are not just the contracted, agitated person we believe ourselves to be. We may remember too that our capacity for joy is too important to forget, and for capacity to deepen it needs care and attention. We are sensual beings and sensual joy is not to be disdained; it teaches us much about our heart's capacity for joy.

Nature is a remarkable ally in teaching us the simplicity of gladness. In moments when joy seems far away from us, we can remind ourselves to step outside, go into a garden, a park, even in the midst of a city, turn our eyes to the sky and simply stop, listen, and breathe. Let your senses simply attend to the clouds moving through the sky, hear the rustle of the wind in the tree branches, see the light on the grass. What is it for us to sense without words, receiving the natural world with sensitivity? We learn to allow ourselves a moment of wonder, knowing the seasons of nature; their beginnings and their endings are mirrors of the seasons of our own lives. In stillness we sense what it is to receive the world, to listen, to see, and to attend, and we make room for joy. The empathy so central in the cultivation of compassion is equally pivotal in the cultivation of joy. In the face of the lovely we sense the trembling of our heart, the capacity to be touched by what is before us and to respond with gladness.

In the teaching of awakening the cultivation of joy, the gladness that is spoken about is inwardly generated, born of awareness, our willingness to be intimate with all things and of understanding and uprooting the patterns of our hearts that obstruct and stifle the joy and gladness possible for us. We are invited to radically transform our understanding of joy. Life brings many joyful moments, yet if our hearts are closed and contracted, these moments do not touch us. For joy to be central in our lives and our way of being, in the world of unpredictability and uncertainty, we are invited to cultivate an unobstructed heart. In meditative training we are taught to cultivate a mind that is clearly present in this moment, to calm our habits of distractedness and learn to make our home in stillness. This is not just about becoming more concentrated, although the benefits of an unforced collectedness of mind are invaluable. We cultivate stillness because the still mind and heart are the source of joy, just as great rivers begin in a simple spring.

A student spoke of the emotional aftermath he experienced after losing his job. For weeks he said,

> I floundered in an ocean of shame, feelings of failure and bleakness. What would get me out of bed in the morning? I obsessively scoured the vacancy ads online and in the newspapers. It was if I had lost "myself," my identity and my worthiness. One morning I woke up and it was different than the morning before. I heard the birds begin to sing as dawn broke. I took my coffee into the garden and realized how long it had been since I had been able to do such a thing in an unhurried way. I was there to get my children up for school and share breakfast with them. I had never done this before. I became acutely aware of all of the lost moments in my life, the moments I had never been part of. There was a deep sense of a new beginning, a present filled with possibilities.

Teachers speak of a "sacred idleness," an endangered art. Joy needs space and room to emerge.

Tasting this inwardly generated joy, born of stillness, has the power to radically alter our relationship with life. We appreciate the moments of delight and happiness that come to us, and deeply know that there is nothing we can gain, possess, or achieve that can offer the same depth of joy that is inwardly born, not dependent on ideal conditions. We are able to step back from the relentless pursuits of objects and experiences, no longer investing them with the power to make us happy and satisfied. We are no longer hostage to the world of conditions, no longer governed by need. In discovering the roots of joy inwardly, we no longer demand of the world, of people, and of events to satiate us and relieve us of distress. Joy as an ennobling quality of the heart is not an episodic joy, triggered by pleasant events and experiences, but a way of abiding, the home of an awakened mind.

Throughout time the great spiritual traditions encourage us to take our seat in stillness. My earliest teacher advised us to find a secluded place with long views to meditate in. The discipline of learning to cultivate a collected mind, firmly established in the present moment, is challenging but an indispensable dimension of the path of cultivating joy. We take moments to disentangle from the world—the world of "doing" and the world of preoccupation—and the heart begins to calm. Over centuries students of awakening have taken themselves to mountaintops, deserts, and secluded caves to discover a joyful and free heart. The Buddha's instructions in meditation invariably begin by encouraging students to take their seats in an empty hut or at the roots of tree and to "disentangle from the world and establish themselves in mindfulness and in solitude." In our contemporary culture we may realistically feel that we do not have the luxury of seeking out an empty cave or leaving our lives in search of seclusion. We may be deeply committed to a life of engagement, with a world in dire need of compassionate human beings. We may not feel called to a hermit's life, yet each of us has a little bit of a nun or a monk within us. We know the value of stillness. Solitude nurtures our heart and simplicity gladdens our mind.

Tasting joy requires discipline; it does not require us to disengage with life. The discipline involved in cultivating joy is not a discipline of forcing or striving; it is a discipline of kindness. How easily we put the care of our own heart at the very bottom of our list of things to do. Making room for joy asks us to learn how to pause and rest in the busyness of our days, to use our sense doors wisely to see and listen wholeheartedly. To make time and space for stillness is to make time and space for appreciation and gladness. Joy does ask us to disentangle from the world of anxiety and relentless busyness. One of the classical teachers, Patrul Rinpoche, said, "Preoccupations do not end until the moment we die. They end when we put them down. This is their nature." For the seeds of inwardly generated joy to begin to emerge, we are all asked to establish ourselves in mindfulness and sensitivity. The meditative disciplines available to us are the doorway to discovering the joy of stillness. The collected mind and the calm heart developed through the formal disciplines of meditative training allow us to discover a way of being in each moment that is imbued with a quiet gladness, in which there is a deep sense of sufficiency.

Obstructions

As a significant aspect of cultivating a liberated and awakened heart, we undertake a genuine investigation of what obstructs joy. We are invited to turn our attention to all the moments in our day that are bereft of joy. In the light of a mindful investigation, we begin to see the patterns and tendencies operating in our hearts that lead to distress. It is this understanding that is the beginning of a path and cultivation that lead to the end of distress, to peace, and to joy. Joy is concerned with two primary areas of insight. The first of these is to awaken to the ways we abide not in freedom, but in an inner culture of lack and insufficiency. The second is to begin to explore the underlying pattern, often unconscious, of perpetually position-ing our "self" in relationship to other "selves"—seeing ourselves as better than another, worse than another, or the same as another, the repeated tendency to judge and define ourselves in comparison to others. These two domains of confusion stifle our capacity for joy and create and re-create distress. There is no shortcut to joy; we do not bypass ourselves on the way to liberation. With mindfulness, kindness, and compassion, we find the courage to meet ourselves, to be intimate with our own hearts, including the most difficult parts of ourselves we are prone to ignore and neglect.

The culture of insufficiency is a powerful ideology that sabotages our capacity for joy and freedom. On a daily basis we are bombarded with messages from the media, advertising, and social expectations that repeatedly tell us we are lacking and insufficient. Models and images of perfection abound, yet perfection remains endlessly elu-sive. We absorb and internalize the demands to be different from who we are—more attractive, more successful, more competent, all deliv-ering the underlying message that this is the way to become more acceptable and loveable. We can feel impoverished inwardly, despite all that we become, possess, and achieve. We hear the inner voices that tell us we do not have enough, are not good enough, that we are imperfect and unlovable. The ideology of insufficiency is a personal and collective belief that generates much of the unhappiness, agitation, and depression that can govern our lives and hearts.

There is much that is sacrificed on the altar of the ideology of insufficiency: stillness, generosity, at times ethics and freedom. Governed by the gnawing sense of incompleteness, we turn outwardly, looking to the world, other people, and experiences for affirmation, gratification, and a solution to discontent. It is an insatiable quest; we have temporary moments of satisfaction and feel elated and even successful. A goal is achieved, an object possessed, an appetite sated, and we relax into a moment of respite from the driving forces of insufficiency and lack that compel us into a world of restlessness and anxiety. All too soon, we find our eyes once more prowling the world for something else to make us happy, to soothe the background murmur of discontent. With our thoughts we lean into the future as the ground where we will discover a perfect moment of happiness. We find ourselves turning away from the moment as it is, toward the moment where life will be as we imagine "it should be."

The Buddha described this as an unquenchable thirst, the craving that is insatiable and has no end. The felt sense of the culture of lack is discontent that is translated into agitated action and thinking in pursuit of a contentment that can never be the lasting outcome of craving. In Buddhist psychology, craving—this unquenchable thirst—is seen to be the primary origin of distress. In confusion, we employ craving as the means to bring distress to an end. If we look carefully at our minds in a single day, it can be a difficult revelation to see how much of our energy, thoughts, and actions are in the service of achieving primarily pleasant experiences and avoiding the unpleasant. The pleasant experience, in the externalization of happiness, is mistaken for joy. It is a poor substitute. We are not invited to judge or condemn the cycles of agitated, craving activity in our lives, but to learn to pause and ask ourselves where enduring joy is to be found. If joy is not to be found here, in this moment, with all its imperfections, then where else would it be found? The Buddha spoke not of transcending the world with all its difficulties, but transcending distress and its roots. When craving grips our hearts, contentment feels far away. When contentment is the ground of our hearts, imperfection is embraced without triggering craving or aversion.

The second dimension of understanding that joy is born of is the clear awareness of the ways that the ideology of "self" unconsciously and subtly distorts our capacity to rest in genuine inner ease and happiness. A primary governing principle in human relationship is the ongoing way that we position our self in relation to others—being superior to another, inferior to another, or the same as another. Initially this can sound vague and innocuous, yet it is a deeply embedded pattern that can govern our lives and has the power to deny joy. Many of the travesties that have scarred human history rest upon this positioning, both individually and collectively. Genocide, war, prejudice, class systems, and abuse rest upon the belief of being superior to others. The perpetuation of low expectations, generational failure, and domestic violence can rest upon the toxic interaction of one person's belief in being superior meeting with another's belief in being inferior.

Positional "selfing," the ways we see ourselves in relationship to others, can determine whom we see as a friend and who is our enemy. It can govern our aspirations, what we believe to be possible for ourselves, and what we believe to be impossible. It is an underlying ideology that can shape our desire to be invisible, to live in the shadows of life, or to be assertive and confident. It may determine whether we are silent or articulate, whether we reach for horizons or settle for limitations. It is an underlying view of ourselves that has the power to shape our lives. What is it that guides us to take our seat at the back of the hall in the shadows or be visible in the front row? What makes us believe that liberation is possible for others but not for ourselves? What makes us keep silent even when there is much we have to offer? What drives us to feel the compelling need to impress others? What leads us to believe we have no capacity to transform our hearts or to compulsively strive to succeed? Why do we feel the need to find flaws even in people we admire so that we can identify with them more easily? Beneath many of the compulsions in our lives, we see the shadowy views of our self as being inferior, superior, or the same as others.

These underlying distortions of self-view have their roots in the early shaping of identity. If we are praised and encouraged throughout our lives, we may not only feel more confident but tend to look down upon others and dismiss them. The shadow companion of confidence, sometimes called its "near enemy," is a quality of pride that rests upon believing ourselves to be superior to others. We become prone to defending our position of superiority by defining ourselves by our roles, our possessions, and our achievements. Alongside this view lives the ongoing whisper of fear—the fear of losing all that we rest upon to support our sense of superiority. Self-protection becomes a primary compulsion in our lives.

If I believe myself to be inferior to you, my psychological and emotional world will feature the ongoing story of self-judgment, comparing, and envy. I may find myself searching for imperfection in others to ease, even a little, the pain of believing in my own imperfection. Gripped in this view of imperfection, life becomes limited, aspiration fails, and impossibility governs our lives. The ideology of incompleteness and insufficiency is endlessly reinforced as we perceive others to be happier, more perfect, and better than ourselves. Despair and depression, frustration, and bitterness become emotional patterns embedded in our hearts.

If I see myself as being the same as everyone else, my mind will incline toward cynicism and doubt. I will find it difficult to celebrate the happiness of others, needing them to be swimming in the same soup of difficulty and unhappiness as myself. I will doubt the altruism or generosity of another, feeling it must be a cover for the same self-absorption I experience. I would perhaps find it difficult to truly admire another for his or her kindness and compassion because to do so would expose me to feelings of inadequacy. The ideology of sameness can superficially feel comforting. It relieves me of the need to aspire to greatness; it can justify the waterfall of judgments we impose upon others and exempt me from the need to see beneath the surface of the views and conclusions I hold about myself and others. The most toxic element in the ideology of sameness is the erosion of confidence and aspiration. The Buddha suggested that a person without confidence is like a person in a boat who has everything but the oars.

The cultivation of joy is an indispensable element in our lives and path of awakening. We seek to understand what it means to rest in a joyful heart that is not just an episodic happiness. We learn to cultivate joy, rooted in understanding and uprooting the obstacles to joy. In one of the early texts, the Buddha taught, "Live in joy, in love even among those who hate. Live in joy, even among the afflicted. Live in joy even among the troubled. Know the sweet joy of the way."[1] He went on to say that it is a disciplined heart that knows true joy, placing joy directly into the context of a consciously cultivated quality and path.

Integrity

The first foundation of joy is integrity, just as it is the cornerstone that underpins the entire path of awakening. In the Buddhist tradition, it is described as the "bliss of blamelessness," a term that sounds very grandiose. In truth it is very simple. Integrity is not a set of rules laden with value judgments of right and wrong, good and bad. The Buddha described integrity as thoughts, words, and acts rooted in kindness and compassion. An ethical life is based on a deep awareness of the roots of our thoughts, words, and acts and whether they contribute to distress or are in the service of bringing distress, alienation, fear, and struggle to an end. We learn to live with a deep awareness that just as our hearts, minds, and lives are deeply affected by the thoughts, words, and acts of others, so too do we leave our own imprint on life with the thoughts we think, the words we speak, and the actions we engage in. We come to know that when our thoughts, words, and acts are driven by fear and ill will, they are compulsive and reactive and leave many echoes in our own minds of regret, shame, and guilt. Moments of compulsive, reactive thinking, speaking, and acting tend to be the most unconscious moments in our lives; they are also the moments we suffer the most and have the most harmful impact upon the world.

Thought, speech, and action rooted in care and compassion leave few traces behind in our own minds but can make a profound contribution to the well-being of another. Motivated by the deep aspiration to bring suffering to an end, we make mindful choices about the thoughts, words, and acts we engage with, out of care for the well-being of all. We know that our safety, peace, and happiness cannot be abstracted from the safety, peace, and happiness of all beings. This is the joy of blamelessness: to live without regret, to live in a way in which no one fears us, and to be trustworthy in all that we do. Integrity is referred to as being the guardian of our hearts and the guardian of the world.

Individuals and communities around the world commit themselves to a life of integrity and a life of joy each day. The forms and words differ, but the essence is the same, to live in a way that protects our hearts and the well-being of the world. It is a commitment to the "bliss of blamelessness," a life without regret and shame. One form of this commitment is expressed in the following:

Knowing the interwoven nature of our lives,
I undertake the commitment to refrain from harming living beings
and to protect the well-being of all
I undertake the commitment to refrain from taking that which is
not freely given and to practice generosity
I undertake the commitment to refrain from sensual and sexual
misconduct and to respect all beings
I undertake the commitment to refrain from false and harmful
speech and to be truthful, honest, and skillful in my speech
I undertake the commitment to refrain from taking substances that
lead to heedlessness and to treasure the clarity of my own mind.

In early Buddhist teachings these commitments are referred to as the five gifts we offer to ourselves. They are the gifts each of us can offer to the world.

Appreciation

The second foundation of joy lies in cultivating and establishing our capacity for appreciation. From the perspective of evolutionary science, we are hardwired to primarily perceive that which is threatening, imperfect, and broken. It is a negative bias of the mind that helped to ensure our survival in early human development and serves some limited value today in helping us to get out of the way of a runaway bus and to skillfully protect ourselves and others. As a default mechanism it is a bias that becomes an emotional habit that stifles appreciation and joy. We step into a garden and find our attention drawn to the weeds, barely noticing the early green shoots of the bulbs. We find ourselves focusing on the flaw in the picture frame before we remind ourselves to look at the beauty of the painting. We return home from work ready to recount to our partner all that has gone wrong in our day, hardly speaking of all that has gone well. Sitting in meditation our aching knee and intrusive thoughts preoccupy us; we barely notice the parts of our bodies that are well. We think a lot about the people we dislike, at times more than we think of those we love. When reflecting on our lives, the difficult memories and experiences take center stage in our attention.

There is an old Chinese saying, "Write your sorrows in sand and etch your joys in stone." It is an invitation to us to reverse the corrosive pattern that inclines us to write our joys in sand, easily forgotten, and to etch our sorrows in stone. Mindfulness teaches us to reclaim our capacity for appreciation. We learn to cultivate many moments when we pause, step out of our busyness and our stories, and truly see what is before us, to listen wholeheartedly, to be touched, and to make room for joy. We sit in meditation, caring for what is broken and difficult in our bodies and minds, and learn to give equal attention to all that is well. We learn to notice the moments in our day when our hearts are not governed by agitation or clinging. Brushing our teeth, we simply brush our teeth. We bring a singular attention to eating, to walking, to feeling the touch of the breeze on our cheek, and we sense the ease, the sense of appreciative joy, in those moments. Rather than glossing over the small acts of generosity we offer, the small words of gratitude and kindness we speak, and the gestures of care we engage in, we learn to honor and celebrate those moments, discovering a taste of joy.

Appreciation rests upon reclaiming an innocence of perception. We see a small child chortling with delight while hold a wriggling worm in his or her hand for the first time, endlessly fascinated with jumping off the same step over and over, and we marvel at a child's capacity for wonder. Joy is concerned with reclaiming that capacity within ourselves, to be able to see anew. It is so clear to us that when our eyes are tired, the world appears bleak. When our hearts are jaded and desensitized, the world becomes colorless and flat. The sensitive, mindful heart perceives value and worth in all things. It does not rely upon drama or intensity to feel awake and alive, but draws upon receptivity, stillness, and a present-moment wholeheartedness.

There is a powerful link between mindfulness and joy and the effect it has upon perception. Perception is a necessary function of consciousness. It is perception that allows us to know the world—that guides us to sit appropriately on a chair rather than endeavoring to sit on a shrub. Perception takes us home to the right address, lets us know our children, and helps us navigate our way safely through the world. Learning to be more intimate with the nature of our mind, we begin to see how perception so quickly moves from being navigational and appropriate into a process that distorts our seeing and our responses to all that we see, hear, feel, touch, and sense. Someone who has hurt us in the past walks into a room; we see the person and feel the flood of memory and associated hurt. We do not see the person as he or she is now; we make our home in our story about him or her. We have frozen the person into an image of being the insensitive, harsh person we do not want to be near. A student returned to a retreat center overlooking the Swiss Alps she had loved the previous year, partly in hope of recapturing the delight she had found in the panoramic views only to remark, "It's not as beautiful as I remembered." We see how quickly we surround sights, sounds, smells, tastes, and touch with association and memory. Perception becomes loaded with reflexive liking and disliking, with labels of good and bad, with fear and anxiety. Perception, distorted, organizes our world emotionally—into friend, enemies, the desirable, and the undesirable. Enchanted by our habits, which are triggered by perception, we rarely see anything anew, and wonder drains from our life. The past is again and again superimposed upon the present. People become fixed for eternity, seen through the images and memories we layer upon them. Experiences, events, and even ourselves become fixed and rigid in our images and thoughts about them.

Mindfulness teaches us to weaken the link between perception and the underlying tendencies and judgments that arise. Superimposing our memories and associations upon all things serves to make the world familiar and known and thus have the appearance of being safer and more certain. It is a process that leaches from our lives the capacity to live this moment fully, to respond to the present freshly, and to appreciate what is. With mindfulness the person who hurt us in the past walks into the room and we may feel the ancient hurt arising. We care for that hurt but also begin to sense the possibility of not being captured by that hurt. Perhaps the person is no longer the person he or she was; perhaps I am no longer the person I was. One of my early teachers taught, "The thought of your mother is not your mother." We could apply the wisdom of those words to all events and people we encounter in this life and to ourselves: "My thought of myself is not myself."

We return to the mountains, not expecting to repeat a past emotional experience but with the willingness to see the unfolding vista of the present. Wonder is found in not knowing, rarely in familiarity. Appreciating what is rather than abiding in what was makes room for joy and wonder. This is no simple task; it requires a profound commitment to being awake in all the moments of our life. It is a commitment to a path of waking up, to liberating all moments from the ties of history, enabling us to see anew and to respond in new ways to our life. We do not need to travel to exotic destinations or chase novel experiences to find joy; we can learn to attend to where we are with new eyes and a receptive heart rooted in not knowing.

The neurologist Oliver Sacks, recovering from a leg injury, wrote about the joy discovered in his enforced stillness as he sat on a stone seat in his garden to light his pipe, saying,

> I had never had the leisure to light a pipe before, or not, it seemed to me, for fourteen years at least. Now suddenly I had an immense sense of leisure, an unhurriedness, a freedom I had almost forgotten —but which now it had returned, seemed the most precious thing in life. There was an intense sense of stillness, peacefulness, joy, a pure delight in the "now," freed from drive or desire. I was intensely conscious of each leaf, autumn-tinted, on the ground, intensely conscious of the Eden around me. I felt like Adam beholding a new world with wonder. I had not known, or had forgotten, that there could be such beauty, such completeness in every moment.[2]

· THE PRACTICE ·

INTENTIONALLY BRING MINDFULNESS to a simple journey you make regularly: the walk to work, the trip to do errands, the time spent on a train. Commit yourself to stillness and to being whole-heartedly present. Bring your attention to simply seeing wholeheart-edly—whatever sights are present, noticing their colors and shapes, mindful of the sun on the ground or the rain washing over the leaves. Sense how your mindfulness illuminates the world of the moment. See with sensitivity; breathe with sensitivity. Allow yourself to be touched and gladdened by the simple moments of loveliness, part of each of our days.

Contentment

Contentment is one of the key cornerstones of joy. So much of life is spent leaning forward into the next moment with our plans, our anticipations, and our expectations. We wait for one thing to be over and something else to begin, looking for the better and more fulfill-ing moment. Momentum and drive are seen to give meaning to life.

Our hopes and dreams capture our attention, and we live in wait for a future joy. We are prone to boredom and enchanted by excitement and intensity. Contentment we may see as the reward for fulfilling our desires and the multiplicity of needs that haunt our lives. In the addiction to intensity, we may even see contentment as undesirable, a state of stupor without meaning or direction. The kind of contentment that is spoken of in the fabric of joy is not passive, not a bovine quality of contentment, like cows grazing in a field, where we resign ourselves to a life of routine and dullness. It is not a surrender of creativity, vitality, or direction; rather it is the ground of all genuine vitality and creativity.

A contented heart is a heart that is at peace with itself. The circumstances and conditions of our lives do not have to be perfect for us to know contentment, the art of resting within what is. Contentment is not the absence of the difficult and challenging, but the absence of our resistance and argument with the difficult and challenging. We find contentment is the mind that is a friend, a place of refuge and confidence. In many spiritual traditions contentment is the first training of early monastics. Living a life where their very survival relies upon the generosity of others, they learn to be content with whatever food is offered, whatever clothing is given, and whatever accommodation is provided, or even if none is provided at all. In the monastic life, the capacity to abide in inner contentment is the central factor in whether their life is one of deprivation or richness. The central teaching in the cultivation of contentment is no longer agreeing to the world of conditions, whether it is food, clothing, or experiences, being the gatekeeper of our inner happiness and freedom. The difficult neighbor does not hold the implicit power to make us unhappy, the ideal vacation does not hold the key to our happiness. Happiness and unhappiness are born within.

One spiritual tradition advises practitioners to pause in every moment of discontent and to ask themselves, "What in this moment is lacking?" Asking this question of ourselves in moments of discontent may provoke a long list of what we feel to be lacking and needed in order for us to be happy, joyful, and contented. We can be discontented with our life and with ourselves. We tell ourselves we need a different body, mind, relationship, and life to be at peace. The list of how other people need to change and the conditions of our life to be altered feels endless. Inner discontentment will consistently generate the list that has no end. We can go through life preoccupied with what we do not have or have never received.

Contentment is not a denial of the deep pain of feeling there is not enough love, support, or acceptance in our lives. Yet here we are in the only life we can live, choosing moment to moment where our hearts will abide, in resentment and deprivation or in contentment. Learning to pause in moments of discontentment, we begin to appreciate that perhaps we have all that we need in this moment for kindness, compassion, and contentment to grow. In the direst circumstances people learn to meet their life not with aversion, but with compassion and poise, and contentment deepens. So too does our capacity to respond effectively to all that is truly unacceptable. Contentment is concerned with bringing to an end the suffering of a heart that seeks perfection in a life that is intrinsically imperfect in its changing and unstable nature. Contentment teaches that we are the gatekeepers of our own hearts and the peace we can discover within them. Contentment is not weakness but strength; we learn one of the key teachings of awakening, to abide in the changing conditions of the world.

There is both a creative and a destructive aspect to discontentment. In the face of our most repetitive and habitual reactions, we can be deeply and sometimes wisely discontented. We do not want to feel so trapped in ways of being that are painful and confining. Resignation and judgment are aspects of a destructive discontentment that serves only to perpetuate the closed feedback loops of aversion, narrative, and despondency. Passivity and hopelessness are symptoms of destructive discontentment. We look at the world with all its ills and descend into helplessness, believing we can make no difference. We look at our own chaotic and turbulent hearts and believe we cannot change; we surrender to despair and seek distractedness. The near enemy of contentment is inertia, which leads us to disengage from life.

There is also a response born of knowing the landscape of our own hearts that is a creative discontentment. A friend remarked that undertaking the path of being mindful of his own mind was akin to volunteering to endure one insult after another, as he saw the repetitive nature of many of his thoughts and reactions. Yet it was that very awareness that inspired him to persevere, to cultivate the ennobling qualities of kindness, compassion, and equanimity. There was joy in seeing the hold of those patterns of reactivity begin to loosen. It is creative discontentment that leads us to say no to the unacceptable, to commit to uprooting suffering and its origins, and to set ourselves on a path dedicated to the awakening of our world.

· THE PRACTICE ·

TAKE SOME MOMENTS to be still, allowing your body and mind to settle into this moment. Sense the life of your body, the places of ease and the places of tension. Listen to the life of your mind with its waves of thoughts and images. Notice the tone of the thoughts—those that are lovely and those that are flavored with discontentment. Bring a simple question into the quietude. What in this moment is lacking? What is being asked of me for contentment to be present?

Confidence

There is joy in seeing the calming and the falling away of aversion, fear, and doubt. There is joy in discovering we are just a little less judgmental, impatient, or agitated. The great political and social transformations in human history have been born of creative discontentment. No longer willing to accept the unacceptable that divides human beings from one another—injustice, poverty, and oppression—we cultivate the ways to bring about change. Little transformation has been born of rage and hatred; much has been born of understanding and compassion. We learn to celebrate and honor our aspirations, efforts, and courage to liberate our hearts and the world from the causes of pain. The Buddha once said, "This is a path of happiness, leading to the highest happiness and the highest happiness is peace." We learn not to be so invested in the outcomes of our actions and efforts but to be confident that it is the effort itself that is worthy. Confidence in the path we are walking brings joy, aspiration brings joy, and to know that every moment of care and compassion truly matters brings joy.

· THE PRACTICE ·

CULTIVATING A STILLNESS of body and mind, settle into a posture of wakefulness. Appreciate your willingness to meet the moment however it is. Take a few moments to bring to mind your deepest aspirations and values—the longing to live a wakeful, engaged, and compassionate life. Sense the moments you have embodied those longings in small and large gestures of generosity and care.

Gratitude

Gratitude is one of the building blocks that incline our hearts toward joy. Many spiritual communities will begin their day chanting gratitude for all they have received. Tibetan monks and nuns offer gratitude amid hardship, saying, "Grant that I may be given appropriate difficulties, that my heart of compassion may be awakened." Native American communities mark the falling of the rain, the growing of the grass, the fish in the rivers with songs of gratitude. Gratitude reminds us of the interwoven nature of our lives. Martin Luther King Jr. wrote, "Whether we realize it or not, each of us lives eternally in the red. We are everlasting debtors to known and unknown women and men. When we arise in the morning we go into the bathroom and reach for a sponge which is provided for us by a Pacific Islander. We reach for soap that is created for us by a European. Then at the table we drink coffee provided for us by a South American or tea by a Chinese or cocoa by a West African. Before we leave the house we are already beholden to more than half of the world."

It is helpful for us to pause again and again in our day and to know that our life is the gift of many. This is not sentimental nor a denial of the many hardships of the past and the present. It is about making a choice concerning where we abide and make our home, in resentment or in gratitude. We are grateful to others, and we learn to offer gratitude to ourselves. The many efforts we make, the moments we choose to be awake rather than asleep, are worthy of gratitude; we are grateful to our friends and benefactors and at times know that even the most difficult people and events in our lives have been the ones that have encouraged us to take the next step on our path to living a wakeful and compassionate life.

I met a friend I hadn't seen in some time. She had suffered a catastrophic kidney failure and was spending many hours each week on dialysis. She told me that one of the local shopkeepers she knew in only a glancing way had offered her one of his kidneys which had proved a perfect match for her. I saw the immense gratitude in her eyes; inwardly I felt a surge of joy in the simple but profound goodness of another human being. We may not be the recipient of such profound, life-changing generosity, but we learn to be grateful for the food we eat, the kindness of strangers, the air we breathe, and life itself. Joy is not always so far away, and we discover the many ways that we can make room for joy.

Rumi, the great Sufi poet, wrote:

Today like every other day we wake up empty and frightened.
Don't open the door to the study and begin reading.
Take down a musical instrument.
Let the beauty we love be what we do.
There are hundreds of ways to kneel and kiss the ground.

· THE PRACTICE ·

DEDICATE SOME MOMENTS to stillness and receptivity, allowing your mind and body to calm. Amid all the challenges of life, remember the many blessings that sustain us. With gratitude, remember the many people who have supported and sustained us through our lives. With gratitude, remember the moments of beauty and loveliness of the natural world. With gratitude, appreciate whatever measure of health we have. With gratitude, remember the generosity of others. With gratitude, remember whatever measure of safety and well-being we have. With gratitude, remember our capacity to touch the lives of others with care and love.

Laying the foundations of joy in our hearts, we can begin to turn our attention to the specific dimension of joy highlighted in the teaching of the brahma viharas of the immeasurable qualities of the noble abidings. *Mudita* is the empathic or appreciative joy that celebrates the happiness and good fortune of the people we meet in our lives. The heart that is freed from envy, resentment, covetousness, and discontentment begins to taste the boundless generosity that can truly rejoice in another's well-being. Our neighbors go on vacation while we stay home and clean the garage, and we are genuinely happy for them. Our friend's child surpasses our own in exams, and we celebrate their success. We overhear the laughter of a child, witness lovers embracing, see a bird escape the pursuit of a predator, and our hearts are gladdened.

Just as our hearts can tremble with empathy in the face of pain and distress, our hearts can also tremble in empathy in the face of happiness. We know what it is to feel gladness with another, to feel happiness with another. Appreciative joy does not rely upon dramatic moments but is a quiet celebration of life itself. An eighteenth-century Sinhalese text frames this quality of joy in the following words:

How wonderful you are in your being
I delight you are here
I take joy in your good fortune
May your happiness continue.[3]

Initially these phrases may be heard as sentimental, something we might feel in the presence of a newborn baby or a cuddly kitten. In truth they are the expressions of the deepest generosity, selflessness, and appreciation. These phrases suggest that no one has to earn, merit, or be worthy of appreciation—it is enough that each person is a living, breathing, sensing human being. The phrases and intentions behind them are not concerned with the story of another person, one's history, preferences, or appearance. They are ways of honoring the person before us with all of his or her longings for happiness and safety, all of his or her wishes to be free of pain and distress.

There are two aspects to the intentions articulated in the practice of appreciative joy. "How wonderful you are in your being / I delight you are here" suggests the boundless nature of empathic joy. With mindfulness, friendliness, and compassion, the person before us is seen wholeheartedly, attended to wholeheartedly in all of his or her complexity. We may or may not know the person, but we see, acknowledge, and celebrate each person's life. "I take joy in your good fortune / May your happiness continue" articulates our deepest aspirations that the person before us finds the way to abide in an abiding happiness.

Appreciative joy is not extended only to others but equally to ourselves. We could take some moments to sit quietly and sense how we would respond to someone offering us this unreserved and unhesitating appreciation. We could also explore the responses we would have if we were to offer these intentions to ourselves.

How wonderful I am in my being
I delight I am here
I take joy in my good fortune
May my happiness continue.

We may immediately hear all the voices of objection arising inwardly: "I am not good enough." "I do not deserve this." "This is self-centered." We may feel embarrassed; we may cringe; we may feel aversive and turn away from this inwardly offered appreciation. In speaking about immeasurable friendliness, the Buddha said that we could search the whole world over and not find anyone more deserving of kindness and care than ourselves. This is equally true of appreciative joy. We all have our difficulties in this life; affliction and adversity visit us, yet still we wake up each morning invited to choose where we will make our home—in resentment or appreciation, in generosity or withholding, in joy or bitterness. We decide what we will do with our attention. We learn to care for the difficult without ever losing sight of what is easeful. We learn to attend with compassion and kindness to the array of hardship that visits all of our lives. We learn equally when to pause, to see and listen with sensitivity, and to celebrate in this moment all that gladdens our hearts.

We can learn that a peaceful coexistence between the difficult and the lovely, between sadness and gladness, between adversity and ease is possible for us. Mindfulness, friendliness, compassion, and joy are like different but interwoven melodies that make up a single song. They are not linear but balance and strengthen one another. When the heart becomes raw in the face of pain, we remember to make room for joy. When unworthiness or judgment overcomes us, we remember that our hearts can tremble in empathy for the pain of this, and we can befriend that sorrow rather than turn away. Appreciative joy invites us to widen the circle of our awareness and to be touched by the many small moments of wellness, blessing, and happiness that are part of our days. We find gladness in the midst of the gladness of another, joy in the happiness of another, appreciation for the many ways our lives and hearts are touched by the life and heart of another. Altruistic joy is not born of great and heroic effort, but of learning, moment to moment, to incline our hearts toward empathy, gladness, appreciation, and wakefulness.

FOUR

Equanimity

Equanimity gives selflessness to metta; gives patience, courage, and fearlessness to compassion; guards joy from sentimentality; and brings all the ennobling qualities of the heart together in liberation.

Through cultivating metta we learn the art of standing near to all the events and people in our lives with boundless friendliness. Compassion teaches us to turn toward all things and people, all the sorrow and distress in this life, with a heart that can tremble and respond with an unshakeable commitment to relieve suffering and its causes, to empathize and bring stillness into the chaos of pain. Joy is needed to soften the rawness and painfulness our hearts can experience in their openness to distress, to replenish and restore ourselves. Equanimity is understanding what it means to stand in the midst of all experience with unshakeable balance, to be responsive yet unbroken.

The Pali/Sanskrit word "equanimity" finds a number of different translations that endeavour to capture its meaning: "to look over," "to be a guardian of," to see with patience and as standing in the middle of life with a boundless poise and balance. Some refer to equanimity as a spacious stillness of the heart. In the early texts, equanimity at times is used synonomously with *nibbana*, or "unshakeable liberation." Equanimity does not leave kindness, joy, or compassion behind but is imbued with these qualities which rescue it from indifference or coldness. Like kindness, joy, and compassion, equanimity is not a state but describes a relational way of being with life that rests upon a profound understanding of the intrinsic nature of change, unpredictability, and nonself that is at the heart of all events and experience. In the midst of all of this, the heart can abide, fully liberated from the greed, hatred, and delusion that create suffering and despair.

We already stand in the midst of this life; there is no other place we can stand. We can imagine ourselves at the center of a mandala, surrounded by those we love, those we struggle with, and the countless beings we do not know. We can visualize ourselves surrounded by the "ten thousand joys and sorrows" that touch every human life. Casting our minds back over the past, we sense the river of events that has brought us to this present moment in our lives—the people we have loved and lost, the delights and the disappointments, the acts we have done and left undone, the highs and the lows that have all been part of the fabric of our lives. We look to the future and know the only certainty is our dying; we do not know when or how. We do know we will be asked to engage with this life. We have no power to predict what difficulties and joys the future or even the next moment will bring.

We return to the knowledge that all we are now is the outcome of all we have been and all we have experienced in the past, and the knowledge that all we will be in the future will be the outcome of who and how we are now. Equanimity is not a future state or attainment but a way of engaging with all that this present moment is revealing. Sowing the seeds of equanimity rooted in a deep understanding of the nature of life, we are a participant in shaping our present-moment heart, which is the mother of the next moment.

Widening the field of our attention and concern, we sense all of those around us, those known and unknown, who also stand in the center of their own mandala, at times intersecting with our own and other times never to be known to us. Yet all of our mandalas intersect in the human story of vulnerability, of aging, sickness, and death. We share the human story of a mind possessing the possibility of vast depths of compassion and understanding and the possibility of great despair, fear, and confusion. We share the human longing to be free from pain and sorrow even as we know that our lives will continue to be touched by pain and sorrow. Our human mandalas intersect in our longing to be happy and safe even as we know this cannot always be so. Our worlds intersect in our longing to protect those we love from distress and loss, even as we know that is beyond our power. Equanimity knows the great capacity to embrace this paradox.

The Buddha speaks of untangling the tangle in the Jata Sutta:

A tangle within
A tangle without,
People are entangled in a tangle.
Gotama, I ask you this:
Who can untangle the tangle.
[The Buddha:] A person established in virtue,
Developing discernment and mindfulness,
Ardent and clear.
They can untangle this tangle.
Those whose passion, aversion, and ignorance
Have faded away.
For them, the tangle is untangled.[1]

We look at the world around us with all its conflicts, cruelty, and human suffering. We stand at the edge of an abyss as our planet and climate are affected by insatiable human consumption. We see the countless lives affected by clashing ideologies and beliefs. The tangle of confusion and conflict seems endless. We look closer to our own families and relationships with their potential for alienation, misunderstanding, and conflict—the tangled knots of hurt. We know we cannot fix it all. We understand the pressing need to bring as much kindness and compassion to the tangles we find ourselves in as possible. We learn that our insistence that life, other people, and ourselves be other than they are has the immediate effect of intensifying the tangle. We can begin to discover an inner stillness and poise in the midst of chaos. This is the gift of equanimity.

We stand upon the shifting sands of life, unpredictable and uncertain. We know this, yet too often we turn away from this simple truth in denial and fear. We know that we cannot choose to have only lovely people in our life, perpetual delightful experiences, endless health and immortality. We know that our world can crumble in a moment—often we do not want to know and thus we invest heroic effort in building defenses against change and uncertainty, which have only the shifting sands as their foundation. Every day our sense doors are flooded with thousands of sights, sounds, smells, sensations, and thoughts. There is little in the world of conditions and change that we can control, no matter how valiantly we endeavor to do so. We also come to know we are not helpless. Every human heart holds the seeds of resilience and balance and the capacity for liberating understanding. The ability to stand with poise in the midst of our lives rests upon bringing those seeds to maturity.

A student told me of her early years practicing meditation in the Himalayan foothills. In search of a peaceful mind she found a secluded hut on the mountainside, but finding the passing locals with their animals too intrusive, she moved farther up the mountain to an ever more secluded hut. Here too she found the wildlife interrupting her meditation and obstructing the peace she sought for. On the move again, she found the most secluded, abandoned animal shelter and moved in. Placing blankets over the windows she finally settled in to meditate and find the peace that had proved so elusive. Little did she know that the tin roof of the shelter was a magnet for the local monkey tribes to play upon. Finding herself outside berating and shouting at the monkeys, it finally dawned on her that peace could never be built upon avoiding life or endlessly endeavoring to control the uncontrollable.

A friend recounted how one of his students, living on a busy, noisy street in Manhattan, hung on the inside of his front door that opened onto the sidewalk a sign that simply said, "Meditation hall." It was a daily reminder to himself that to make his inner world of balance and responsiveness dependent upon a world of ideal conditions was a recipe for defensiveness and discouragement. The external world of conditions and the internal world of our heart are always interrelated but not always interdependent. The invitation of equanimity is to learn to abide in calm in the midst of agitation, to abide in peace in the midst of conflict, to abide in balance in the midst of chaos. It seems to be an impossible task. Yet the size of the task is only ever equal to the size of the moment.

We step into the world of conditions the moment we wake and our sense doors interface with the world. Learning to make our home in kindness, compassion, joy, and equanimity, we are never far from our "meditation hall." As the Buddha taught in one of the earliest texts, the *Dhammapada*, "All experience is preceded by mind, led by mind, and shaped by mind. All that we are arises with our thoughts. With our thoughts we make the world." A world shaped by mindfulness, understanding, and the ennobling qualities of the brahma viharas is a world of freedom.

In the midst of all of this, the life that doesn't go away, we are so easily knocked off balance, overwhelmed, and shattered. At times we feel helpless and lost; at other times we blame life for being unfair. We may be tempted to find refuge in defense or in forgetfulness only to have life remind us time and time again that the only true refuge in this life is to be found in a heart that can meet this life as it is with courage, compassion, and balance. The Buddha once said, "It would make no sense for me, a being subject to change, uncertainty, and death, to try to find refuge in that which is also subject to change, uncertainty and death." Understanding this deeply we cease our frantic search for certainty and predictability; we calm our frantic endeavors to control the uncontrollable and learn to be still in the midst of the vicissitudes of life with a heart that is open and willing to embrace all moments with poise and spaciousness.

Equanimity is a pathway, a way of being present, and a seed we cultivate, an ongoing journey of investigation. Just as life does not stand still, frozen in time, exempt from change, equanimity is equally fluid, a responsive way of meeting our shifting life, our changing body and mind, and all of the events we are asked to embrace. It is not developed in the most sublime and peaceful moments in our lives but in the moments we feel most agitated and shattered, most lost and unbalanced. It is a practice of meeting and understanding the uncertainty and unpredictability we so fear and a commitment to the freedom of our own hearts in the midst of it all. The path of equanimity asks us to question whether it is the events and changing conditions of our lives that shatter our hearts or our reactions to them. Is there another way of responding to change, loss, and uncertainty other than with fear and aversion, the demand that life conforms to our wishes and desires, or with dissociation? The path of awakening invites us to develop the profound insight that is the foundation of a heart that can abide in a boundless stability in the midst of the unstable.

The path of equanimity begins with the awareness of the places and moments where equanimity most easily vanishes. Our life is an unceasing, almost unstoppable flow of events, one following on the heels of another. Like a river that emerges from a spring and begins to flow, in the course of the river there are stretches of white water, places of calm followed by rapids, and whirlpools that once more even out only to turn into a waterfall. We can no more stop the river than we can shield ourselves from the events that touch us with their joys and sorrows. We cannot choose to rest only in the peaceful stretches just as we sense the rapids and eddies will also change into something else.

The Worldly Winds

Each of our lives will be touched by what are called the winds of the world. Moments of praise and blame, success and failure, pleasure and pain, gain and loss are woven into every human life. In the light of approval and praise, we glow; in the light of disapproval and blame, we find ourselves ashamed and withering. Understandably we long for acceptance and appreciation—the near enemy of this very human longing is the pursuit of approval and praise. Too easily we place ourselves at the whims of another's words of affirmation. Understandably blame, judgment, and criticism are hard to bear. The near enemy of this pain is to seek for an elusive perfection or to deafen ourselves to feedback from others. Too easily we internalize the anger and aversion of others as being an accurate measure of who we are. We are prone to personalize both praise and blame, describing ourselves by them and subjecting ourselves to elation and despair. Equanimity disappears in the contractedness of identification.

The wonderful meditation we finally achieved, the love we were sure would last forever, our health and youth—all are delighted in, yet all will change, and we are asked to meet the bleak landscape of disappointment and feelings of failure. Life continues to teach us the hard lessons of letting go. Culturally we are told that our worth as a human being is defined by our successes and that failure is unacceptable, an indictment upon our worthiness. During the recent recession, rates of mental illness and suicide skyrocketed. We strive to become the kind of person who is immune to failure and to fearfully defend our successes. Culturally we are taught that success opens the door to love, acceptance, and reward, whereas failure sentences us to the shadows of life. We can become frantic in our search to secure our well-being through success and possession and come to fear the loss of that certainty, believing it will sentence us to a life of invisibility and meaninglessness. We can even believe that equanimity will be the outcome of securing success rather than found through the willingness to be equally near the highs and the lows of life.

Our hearts are touched and gladdened by the moments of pleasure and delight the world offers to us. The simple joys of the sunlight touching our face, the great joys of a newborn child, the wonderful art, music, and poetry available to us gladden our hearts and enrich our lives. We love health, lovely emotions, and pleasant thoughts. We do not open so easily to the moments of pain—the unexpected illnesses, the difficult emotions, the repetitive thoughts, the vexing sights and sounds. The sounds of the birds outside the window are drowned out by the roar of the garbage truck. A delightful fantasy or plan is replaced by a nightmarish obsession. Our health falters and at times we become weary and bored with what we previously delighted in.

We develop the habit of leaning toward and pursuing the pleasant, flinching from the unpleasant, and doing all we can to arrange the conditions of our lives in ways that protect us from pain. We rarely appreciate that our very pursuit of pleasure makes us increasingly intolerant of pain and binds us to a life of agitation and anxiety. Equanimity holds within it a quality of resilience that is not an armoring against the winds of the world, but born of inner strength and poise. We are affected deeply by the unexpected changes and events of both the lovely and the unlovely. We will bend before the force of those winds but learn to return to uprightness. Cultivating our capacity for balance, we learn to meet the many small moments of discomfort that are part of our daily experience without flinching or turning away, discovering it is possible to surround discomfort with a calm stillness. We discover the capacity to meet the many small lovely moments of our day with a quality of appreciation that is not distorted by our desire to possess and maintain the pleasure of the lovely.

Experiences of gaining and losing are woven into the rhythm of our lives. We gain stability and security, money and stature. We gain respect and stability. Many of the achievements of our lives are born of skillful effort and dedication and are to be honored. We also lose a great deal. We are separated from people we love; our livelihoods disappear; we face the loneliness of friendships that change or disappear. We lose our youth and vitality; we gain a newfound peace in the midst of aging. A mother told the story of the heartache of being informed that her son had died in the Asian tsunami. The following week she received a postcard from him saying, "I am in heaven, this is the best time of my life." There are unexpected moments of stillness, unpredicted moments of depression. Equanimity is a teaching not only of poise but of grace, a deep knowing that life will not stand still for any of us and that to rely upon stability is a recipe for agitation and anxiety.

In the midst of all of this we still breathe, our hearts beat, we go from morning to night and remain present and alive. We ask ourselves how our hearts can continue to absorb the ongoing, changing stream of events without being shattered. We see the ways in a single day that our minds swing between highs and lows, elation and despair, fear and confidence. Equanimity pivotally teaches us to meet this river of uncertain and changing events equally with respect, yet without being governed by them. The Buddha said, "Praise and blame, gain and loss, pleasure and pain, success and failure are the eight worldy winds. They ceaselessly change. As a mountain is unshaken by the wind, so the heart of a wise person is steady amidst all the changes on this earth."

A woman told me of the moment she "realized" she had terminal cancer. She had received the diagnosis of inoperable ovarian cancer some weeks earlier. She told how her learning of the diagnosis was followed by a wave of frantic activity. She hoped she would be the rare "miracle" survivor; she sought out healers. She became lost in worry and wondered what she had done wrong to warrant this terrible illness. She found herself sitting on the rocker on her porch one evening, and the moment of a startling "realizing" came to her. She said,

> It was as if my world tilted on its axis. I looked at the stars and heard the hoot of the owl. It was as if all separation between my inner world and the outer world dissolved. Suddenly there was a great stillness, the waves of worry calmed and instead of being lost in the endless litany of "why is this happening to me," I found myself able to meet the reality of my dying. There was acceptance but also a profound dynamic aliveness, every breath was precious, every sound heard as it had never been heard before. I glimpsed something sacred, beyond words. I knew stillness could be my true home.

Equanimity asks for the wisdom of a buddha. In cultivating boundless kindness, joy, and compassion, we begin to sense the ways in which craving and aversion, pursuit and refusal, are toxic elements that create and re-create distress in our lives. The path of equanimity deepens this understanding and has the power to uproot the causes of suffering. It is not only in the outer events and experiences of our lives that we are asked to develop a radical calm and equilibrium, but equally we learn to develop this unshakeable poise within the inner events of our minds and hearts: in the midst of the likes and dislikes, the waves of resistance and wanting, we learn to pause, to sense not only the arising of the waves but equally to allow for their passing. Craving and aversion are agitation; they are compulsive and habitual energies. They rely upon positing within objects, people, and events the implicit power to make us happy or unhappy, sorrowful or elated. Craving and aversion, in positing this implicit power, also posit an independent self-existence in objects, people, and events. In doing so the quality of our hearts and minds is governed and determined by the success of our craving and aversion. We become prisoners of the inevitable highs and lows of every human life; the chains that bind us are the forces of craving and aversion.

In the midst of pleasure and pain, praise and blame, gain and loss, success and failure, we remind ourselves of the possibility of meeting the winds of the world with a calm, still sense of balance. As in the cultivation of kindness, compassion, joy, and equanimity, this remembering is supported by a few simple phrases that aid our return to equanimity in the moments we feel in danger of being overwhelmed or shattered. As always it is helpful to find the words that are meaningful to us, that bring forth the intention to abide in stillness.

· THE PRACTICE ·

IN THE MIDST of a life with its "ten thousand joys and sorrows," we can simply attend to how we are present just now. Allow the body to come to stillness and the mind to settle, attending to the life of this moment, however it is. In the midst of the lovely, in the midst of the difficult, we make our home in our capacity to embrace, include, and care for the well-being of our hearts.

> **May I embrace change with stillness and calm.**
> **May I deeply accept this moment as it is.**
> **May my home be a home of balance and spaciousness.**

Each time we return to an intentional way of being with both the lovely and the unlovely, we are untangling the patterns of aversion and craving that lead us to abandon the moment. Moments of dissociating and abandoning the moment we are in are all moments that undermine our confidence in the freedom of our own hearts. Through flights of aversion, we build fences that make our world a little smaller, telling ourselves we cannot bear this life as it is. Through following patterns of craving, we convince ourselves over and over of the insufficiency of our own hearts. Equanimity teaches us to live as if we were a mountain, touched by the winds of the world but unshaken. We learn to be steadfast, receptive, and committed to freedom. A Zen master was once asked, "What is the secret of your happiness?" He answered, "Complete, unrestricted co-operation with the unavoidable." The unavoidable is our life.

The Winds of Change

The Buddha once said that just as the footprint of the elephant in the jungle is the greatest of all the animals' footprints, so too is the insight into impermanence the greatest of all insights. Understood deeply it is a pivotal insight that has the power to radically transform our hearts and our relationship to life. Can we truly understand that written upon every single thing, event, and person that comes into being, that is born, is the story of its passing and its death? Everything that is built will, in time, collapse. Everything that is joined will, in time, be separated. Everything that is stored will, in time, run out. Every single thing that appears will, in time, fade.

Intellectually we agree with the truth of impermanence. In the passing of events and experiences we dislike, we become enthusiastic advocates of change. The difficult neighbor moves away, an illness passes, an obsession eases, and the sun banishes the rain: we applaud impermanence when it benefits us. It remains challenging to embrace the reality that impermanence will equally touch all that we love and cherish. We despair in the face of losing someone or something we cherish, when our great plans are disappointed, when we no longer have the ability to run like a child, when our hearts are broken by rejection.

Our moments of fame and disgrace, those we love or hate, the pleasure and the pain, the gains and the losses—none of them are graspable; all are held in the embrace of impermanence. Not understanding this deeply, we become lost in craving and aversion and in forgetfulness. Heroic efforts are made to keep, maintain, and possess that which is already passing or to eradicate the things that are equally held in the clasp of change. In teaching impermanence the Dalai

Lama once instructed his students to reflect on all that has already disappeared. The afflictions we thought would last forever, the people we have loved and lost, the identities and passions we assumed would be lifelong—all now are simply a memory. The tens of thousands of thoughts we have had, the emotions we have struggled with, the dreams—all have changed. We could further reflect on what is disappearing right now and what will surely disappear in the future.

Every single thing we sense and experience has a singular message—to let go. We do not always realize how much we rely upon the great and small things in our lives to stay the same for us to feel balanced and poised—until they change. Clinging is an intensification of craving and aversion and is the primary way we turn away from the reality of change. It is the denial that triggers a life of anxiety and restlessness. Core to this anxiety is the central denial of our own mortality. We do not stand outside of the inexorable rhythms of change—one day we too will only live in someone's memory. Nāgārjuna, the great Indian sage, taught,

Life flickers in the flurries of a thousand ills,
More fragile than a bubble in a stream.
In sleep, each breath departs and is again drawn in;
How wondrous that we wake up living still.

Shunryū Suzuki Roshi, a great twentieth-century Zen teacher, once said, "Understanding impermanence is not a rejection of the things of this world, but an acceptance that they pass away." We are not short of opportunities to contemplate impermanence—beginnings and endings, births and deaths, are revealed in a single moment contemplated with awareness. One lesson is stamped upon all things—this too will pass. Understanding the primary truth of change has profound implications. If we are to be free, we are asked to cultivate a mind that is free of grasping. If we are to live this life with grace, we are asked to learn to embrace not only beginnings, but also endings. If we are to love deeply, we learn not to demand that people stand still for us.

Equanimity is deeply rooted in the cellular understanding of impermanence. It does not mean that we do not care, simply that we do not cling. Craving, aversion, and confusion are the conditions that lead to grasping. Metta, compassion, and joy are the conditions of nonclinging and equanimity. We could undertake a simple reflection. We know what it feels like to experience a mind that is imbued with agitation, craving, or aversion. A difficult thought or image arises in this emotional climate and almost immediately puts down roots, begins to grow, and is identified with. Hours later the climate of our mind may change into a more spacious, easeful mind. The same difficult thought or emotion appears yet puts down no roots and passes through. Shouting at ourselves to "let go" is ineffective and dooms us to failure. Cultivating kindness, joy, and compassion gives birth to a mind that is no longer prone to clinging. Understanding impermanence teaches us to stand in the midst of all things with equanimity.

Embracing the reality of impermanence has profound implications for how we live our lives. Reflecting deeply upon the truth of impermanence reveals a kinder way of being in this world with all things and all people. Life is too fleeting to be spent in conflict and argument. Reflecting deeply upon the truth of our own mortality, we find an urgency to live a meaningful, caring, and compassionate life. Understanding impermanence we may become a little disenchanted with the pursuit of ephemeral things and experiences. Absorbing the reality of impermanence focuses our mind on what is truly valuable in this uncertain, changing life. Our capacity to love and care for others, our commitment to ease distress when it can be eased and to be steadfastly present with sorrow that has no solution—both are born of an unshakeable understanding of the reality of change.

Invited to celebrate the sixtieth birthday of a friend, some of us were a little surprised to find ourselves seated before a slab of slate and offered a piece of chalk. It was time to write our own gravestones. No one was tempted to be remembered by all that we had gained, our successes, or by our capacity to avoid the difficult. Sharing our reflections afterward people spoke of their wish to be remembered as someone who had tried to make a difference in this difficult world, who had tried to love and care, and as someone who had lived his or her life as wisely and wholeheartedly as possible. Traditional teachings of awakening highlight the understanding of impermanence as a key insight in awakening an urgency to be awake, to live with compassion, and to be a participant in the awakening of our world. Across the globe nuns and monks begin each day with a collective reflection upon impermanence and their own mortality. This is not a reflection meant to be reserved for monastics. How would our life be changed by a practice such as this? Impermanence, held at the forefront of our consciousness, has the potential to guide us to a life of integrity, appreciation, care, and wakefulness.

Universal Vulnerability

The second crucial dimension of equanimity is the domain of human relationship—the sphere of our lives where we often most feel shattered both by love and hate. We are relational and emotional beings. It is the capacity of our hearts to feel deeply that leads us to love, to care, to be touched by the joy and the sorrow of others, and to reach out to heal and to help whenever we can. Our emotional worlds are the home of our deepest passions and thus our deepest vulnerability. Equanimity is not a pathway of abandoning or subduing the richness of our emotional life—this would be a life of disconnection and dissociation. All of the brahma viharas have only one direction, a life of deeper connectedness. Equanimity is concerned not with emotional flatness but with emotional intelligence and freedom. The wisdom of equanimity teaches us not to subdue our passions but to no longer surround our passions with delusion and intoxication.

We easily become infatuated with both love and hate. To be able to love deeply and receive love is the greatest art of the human heart. Yet we can become infatuated with love, pursuing and grasping it, fearing its loss, or assuming the role of being the perpetual rescuer of others. The infatuation with love leads us to become preoccupied and obsessed with the objects of our passions, and we experience the painfulness not of love, but of intoxication. We invest an implicit power in the person we love to make us happy, feeling our very survival relies upon our love being returned and remaining unchanged. In doing so we cede our inner freedom and sense of inner sufficiency to the person we come to depend upon. Once more we find ourselves fueling the fires and discontentment born of craving and grasping. Our love for others can be distorted into an overprotectiveness, the agitation of trying to keep the tides of unpredictability and change at bay, and an endeavor to be the perfect parent, partner, daughter, or son. We can assume the impossible responsibility of making another person happy. The shadow side of our deep care of another is to try to control that person's world of experience and shield that person from pain and from life itself.

The pathway of cultivating equanimity invites us to ask challenging questions: Can we love without being bound by love? Can we care deeply yet know we cannot totally protect those we care for from pain and sorrow? Can we love without leaning on the person we love to provide the evidence and affirmation that we are worthy and loveable? Can we love without the demands that the person we love make us happy and ensure our well-being? Can we accept that we do not hold in our hands the power to ensure the safety and happiness of those we love most deeply? The Buddha encouraged a path of freedom, learning to abide independently, not clinging to anything in this world yet caring deeply.

Alongside this teaching of liberation is the teaching of deeply knowing that our very life is intrinsically interwoven with the lives of others. Each of our thoughts, words, and acts splinters into thousands of consequences that make an imprint upon the world around us, touching the lives of others. The thoughts, words, and acts of others deeply touch our own life. We cannot determine the skillfulness or unskillfulness of another person's heart. We can take care of the ground that our own thoughts, words, and acts arise from, letting them be born of kindness, compassion, and joy and cultivating the inner balance that can live in the midst of unruly and difficult people without being broken. Our lives, from the moment of our birth, are affected and defined by our relationships. Our emotional maturity and freedom grow in the classroom of a participatory world. Cultivating the wisdom of kindness, compassion, joy, and equanimity, we discover a freedom to participate in this relational world that is no longer distorted by greed, hatred, and confusion, but guided by generosity, balance, and understanding.

We can become as intoxicated with ill will as with love, and the effect is the same. The words and acts of ill will we receive from others affect us deeply. We are wounded by judgment and rejection, hurt by indifference and cruelty. Difficult people will continue to be part of our life; we learn to develop the equanimity and freedom that does not consent to them governing our consciousness and heart. A young woman spoke of the emotional aftermath of being mugged on her journey home one evening. She was shocked but not injured in the attack, yet she said she found herself obsessively replaying the incident in her mind, thinking more about her assailant than the people in her life she most deeply cared about. She found herself becoming hypervigilant and suspicious of everyone she caught sight of on her daily commute home. There came a point when, she said, "I realized that my mugger had come to govern my heart and my life. Not only had my outer freedom disappeared, but also the freedom of my heart." It was a startling realization but equally startling was the understanding that she had the freedom to choose how she was going to hold the memory of the incident in her mind. She found she could meet the thoughts and images as thoughts and images, arising from the past with clarity and with compassion. She found herself being able to hold the thoughts and images of the event as they arose in the present as thoughts and images that could be met without fear. She spoke of the freedom discovered in no longer wishing for a different past. It was a release and a healing into the present.

In ill will we bind ourselves to the person we fear. We avoid and distance ourselves. We find ourselves creating an "other," investing the other with the implicit power to shatter our hearts. In the face of injury or hurt we sense the tendency to seize upon a fragment of another person and mistake it to be the whole. We become preoccupied with an insult, hurt by an act of ill will or indifference, and decide that the person before us is cruel, hateful, or ignorant. A decade could pass before we see the person again, yet the moment our eyes catch sight of that person, we see only the person we have determined him or her to be, unacceptable and intimidating. This selective perception closes the door not only to kindness and compassion but also to equanimity. The "other" becomes frozen in time and space by our fear, and instead of being willing to be equally near all things, we are driven by the desire to distance ourselves.

We cannot change the heart of another; only each person has dominion over the thoughts, passions, and emotions he or she experiences and embodies. Finding the still whispers of balance within our own heart, we can learn not to give so much credibility or authority to the thoughts, words, and acts of ill will we receive from another. These words may not be telling us anything at all true about us; they are saying something about the torment, confusion, and fear of another's mind. Knowing this we learn to rest in the equilibrium of our own heart, able to turn toward the world without fear. Like the grasses that bend before the force of the winds, we still feel but may discover the possibility of not feeling shattered.

If we are fortunate, we will care deeply for many people in our lives. We tend to our families, care for friends in good and difficult times, for aging parents and loved ones meeting their own measure of adversity. There may be many moments of kindness, compassion, and joy; there is also a great need for equanimity. We may see people we care for make choices that harm themselves, or engage in actions and ways of being that bring a waterfall of suffering upon themselves and others. We see people we love become ill, despairing, and helpless in the face of their aging and imminent mortality. We respond as wholeheartedly as we are able and sense the trembling of our hearts in compassion. We commit to doing all that is possible to ease the pain of a loved one. We can also feel the pain of our own powerlessness to fix everything, to make the difficult go away, to heal the pain of a loved one or change the mind lost in confusion. This is the ground in which equanimity and stillness are most needed and often most elusive.

In a practice of equanimity the seeds of intention are planted through the medium of a few simple phrases.

· THE PRACTICE ·

TAKE SOME MOMENTS to settle yourself into an intentional and wakeful posture, sensitive to the life of your mind and body. Expand your awareness to remember the many people who are part of your life just now: those you love, those you struggle with, and the many you do not know. Sense your capacity to care deeply, yet simultaneously know that there will always be limits to the effect we can have upon the heart of another. Sense what it is to rest your attention in a few simple phrases.

> Life is but a play of joy and sorrow
> May I remain unshaken by life's rise and fall
> I care for you deeply
> But you are the parent of your acts and their fruit
> And sadly I cannot protect you from distress.[2]

These few simple phrases capture the heart of equanimity. It is a seed of intention that is planted again and again, each moment of helplessness and despair reminding us of the possibility of returning to a place of wisdom and stillness. We care, but however deep our care, it cannot always protect the person we love from sorrow. The statement "you are the parent of your acts and their fruits" is not comprised of words of indifference or blame but expresses the simple knowledge that just as our thoughts, words, and acts are born of our understanding or our confusion, so too is this true for all beings. Just as we know that as much as others may love and care for us, they do not hold the power to heal our sorrow or change the ways of our hearts. This lies in our hands, and the same is true of another's life and heart.

Faced with the sorrow and pain of those we love, of all in the world, we are asked to make our home in our deepest understanding of the way things actually are. It is the first ennobling truth the Buddha taught: none of us have an exemption from our own measure of sorrow, nor do those we love or those we struggle with. Sorrow is born of a life that is constantly changing, uncertain, and ungraspable. Sorrow is born of living in a matrix of changing conditions, at times coming together in ways that are deeply challenging. Embodying this understanding deeply is what enables us to live in the light of the understandings that free us from despair and resistance. We learn we can inhabit an intentional space of stillness and balance even as our hearts tremble. It is stillness that enables us to reach out, to respond, to heal when healing is possible, and to still know the courage of equanimity that rescues the heart from being overwhelmed by a life that can hold such depths of sorrow.

Martin Luther King Jr. spoke powerfully of the ground of equanimity we can find in the midst of ill will, saying, "Never succumb to the temptation of becoming bitter. As you press for justice, be sure to move with dignity and with discipline, using only the instruments of love." This may sound an impossible task in the midst of the ill will in our world that creates such deep pain and injury. None of us holds the power to make all ill will and distress end; the landscape of hatred, fear, and aversion is vast. We can only take care of our own hearts as we meet the moment we are in. Ill will may have long historical roots, yet it arises in the present. It is in this moment that we plant new roots, in our capacity for courage, kindness, compassion, and equanimity. We learn we can meet the ill will of others and the waves of ill will that rise in our own hearts without heaping ill will upon ill will. We learn we cannot choose what life brings to us but have the freedom to choose how we respond to this unpredictable, uncertain life.

Again it can be helpful to use a few simple words that remind us of our capacity to be steadfast, balanced, and still in the midst of all of our relationships with those dear to us and those we fear.

I care for you deeply but sadly cannot protect you from distress.
You are the parent of the choices you make and their outcomes

and I cannot make those choices for you.
May I rest in care and stillness in the midst of sorrow.

At times the simpler phrase "It is as it is" reminds us to step out of the maelstrom of emotional confusion and of the possibility of returning to a home of greater stillness and balance. Equanimity is a challenging training. In the midst of emotional intensity, it can be helpful to step back and return to a more accessible pathway— cultivating our capacity for kindness, joy, or compassion. The fires of intoxication with love and ill will can burn fiercely; their cooling may rely on our knowing the moments when we are fueling the fires and being able to step out of the flames, even for a moment.

Awakening

The third dimension of equanimity is the fruition of kindness, compassion, joy, and understanding in an unshakeable liberation of the heart. It is the third ennobling truth taught in the path of awakening. There is an end to sorrow, despair, and suffering found in the deepest peace that cannot be broken. It is the blowing out of the fires of greed, hatred, and confusion through profound understanding. The freedom of our heart is embodied in an immeasurable and boundless kindness, compassion, and joy. Johann Wolfgang Goethe wrote,

> I have come to the frightening conclusion that
> I am the decisive element.
> It is my personal approach that creates the climate.
> It is my daily mood that makes the weather.
> I possess tremendous power to make life miserable or joyous
> I can be a tool of torture or an instrument of inspiration.
> I can humiliate or humor, hurt or heal.
> In all situations, it is my response that decides whether a crisis
>   is escalated or de-escalated and a person humanized or
>   dehumanized.

In the teaching of awakening, equanimity is an abiding born of our willingness to meet our life and understand what causes distress and what brings distress to an end. The Buddha was deeply interested in the architecture of suffering and the architecture of the mind that creates and re-creates a world of distress. It is a teaching that asks us to explore deeply how our personal worlds are constructed and built moment to moment with our perceptions, our thoughts, our emotional patterns, and our reactivity. We can go through our lives believing our minds are like a mirror accurately reflecting life as it is. We are at times startled into the realization that instead our minds are the core element in constructing the world of the moment. It is the world we inhabit, react from, and believe to be true.

Years ago teaching in Israel I saw a dog lying outside the office door with eyes closed and a massive growth protruding from the top of its head. I was shocked and horrified by the sight of this apparently desperately ill dog. Those first moments of unhesitating compassion were followed by several hours of intermittently rehearsing all of the things I needed to do to help this poor dog and the ways I perhaps needed to upbraid the kibbutz staff for the neglect of their animals. Returning to the office at lunch I was met by the sight of the dog sitting up wagging its tail and its tumor lying on the ground beside it. It was no more than a desert stone the same color as the dog's fur.

Our world of experience is a very personal world, yet repeatedly we are tempted to assume it is a universal world. Through the processes of sensory information interfacing with perception, memory, emotional association, and thought, the people in our lives are identified as friends, enemies, or those we are simply indifferent toward. Objects are deemed to be wonderful, awful, intrinsically beautiful, or ugly; situations are deemed to be implicitly intimidating or enchanting. Our views of all things and ourselves are given authority and become an absolute truth. We are at times left bewildered when the views or assumptions of another do not accord with our own, the discord easily becoming the source of conflict and alienation.

How many times in our lives are we startled to discover that life is somewhat different from what we assumed? Our views of ourselves or another person are altered by new information or experience. The person we had decided was incorrigibly uncaring reaches out to us with a simple act of generosity. The view we hold of ourselves as being perpetually agitated is altered by an unexpected moment of calm and peace. The heartache we assumed would be with us forever turns into a moment of simple joy. Too often we find ourselves imprisoned by our views and imprisoning the world, ourselves, and others in those same views.

Recently, while eating in a small restaurant, a group of young children began running through the restaurant, squealing and shouting, in the enthusiasm of their game knocking into the tables of other diners. As their volume and excitement increased so too did the palpable tension and irritation levels of the customers in the restaurant. No one it seemed was containing the antics of these children, who seemed unaware of the impact they were having upon others. I could overhear those near me beginning to mutter about "out of control kids" and this "shouldn't be happening." I wondered where their parents were, as they were seated behind a corner out of my line of sight. Peering around the corner I saw a group of young mothers, all of them signing to each other. They could not hear their children, perhaps had never had the joy of being able to hear their children. Any view that I had begun to construct about indifferent parents melted into a place of compassion and empathy. The children were having a wonderful time, their mothers moving unhearing through a hearing world. Soon the children were gathered up, hugged, and they all left. I found myself reflecting with an enhanced awareness on how life is constantly inviting us to question our views and assumptions.

Our world of experience is fluid and ever changing. Each moment our sense doors interface with the world of sensory information, inwardly and outwardly. We are flooded by a cascade of sight, sounds, sensations, taste, smells, and thoughts. They all register in our consciousness and we perceive them. We name the bare sensory data through the medium of perception. The bare sound is identified as a "bird," the sensation as "pain," the smell as a "rose," the sight as a "friend" or an "enemy." We have a name for what is perceived; the name comes to be a way of summing up the reality of what is perceived just as our own name becomes the standard-bearer of who we are or believe ourselves to be.

We cannot do without perception; it is what enables us to navigate our way through life in a functional manner. It is a function of consciousness that enables us to move through life with competence and to know the moment. Navigational perception teaches us to get out of the way of a speeding car and refrain from touching a burning fire. Navigational perception is the useful learning from life that leads us to protect ourselves and others.

Perception also becomes one of the primary building blocks of our world of experience in the moment. Perception travels the same neural pathways as memory. Without mindfulness we become acutely aware of the ways that perception draws upon the past in order to identify and organize the present. The smell of garlic wafting from the kitchen evokes a flood of memories of falling in love in an Italian restaurant. The sight of a person evokes our past experience with that person, lovely or unlovely. A painful sensation in our back takes us into the past world of a life beset by back pain and imaging a future limited by pain. We see someone who has eyes like those of our difficult father, and we are cast back to relive painful childhood memories.

We find our consciousness being overtaken by the world not only of memory but of associated past emotion with those memories. Garlic becomes wonderful; the person we see before us becomes the difficult person we want to avoid; the sensation in our back triggers urgent planning to see our physiotherapist. Perception triggers emotional memory and historical reactions based upon those memories. In a very real way perception without mindfulness is drawing the past into the present, interpreting the present on the basis of past experience. We find ourselves living the present through the filter of the past, repeating the same emotional reactivity and reifying our perceptions to become a truth.

To learn to see something truly anew in this life is an integral part of awakening. Memories and associations arise, but we come to know them as memories and associations that can never tell the whole truth of the moment. In his writing, the linguistic philosopher Ludwig Wittgenstein proposed, "Words deliver us a picture and the picture holds us captive." We come to appreciate that the only thing that keeps anything static in this life is the view that we superimpose. Perhaps one of the greatest acts of compassion is to liberate ourselves, other people, and the world from the views that imprison them. Perception, drawing upon past association, not only organizes our world of the moment but also serves to make that world familiar to us. Our aversions, avoidance patterns, and cravings seem almost predetermined. We know how to react because we know the world, rarely questioning the familiar circles of reactions we walk in.

We learn to rely upon our sense of knowing the world, another person, and ourselves as a form of protection from harm but also from uncertainty. Fear tells us that surprise or not knowing is unsafe. Wisdom tells us that our capacity to deepen as a human being relies upon us being able to rest in not knowing. This is what enables us to learn, to be touched in new ways, and to be responsive rather than reactive. Instead of perpetually superimposing our narrative of the world upon all moments, we learn to cultivate the inner sensitivity and receptivity in which the world can reveal itself to us in the immediacy of the moment. We allow ourselves to be taught, to question, to be touched. We develop the malleability inwardly in which our minds can be changed and our responses to the moment can be radically altered in the light of new experience.

Perception and unquestioned views activate not only memory and association but the underlying patterns of craving, aversion, and confusion that are interwoven with those memories and associations. We find ourselves moving toward or moving away from sensory impressions, people, events, and experiences based upon how we have reacted in the past. It is no surprise that we find ourselves walking in the same closed circles of reactivity and agitation in our life. Equanimity is noticeably absent in the repetitive cycles of reactivity.

In the Honeyball Sutta, the Buddha offered a simple and universal formula through which we can understand and trace the moment-to-moment construction of our personal world. This is not an abstract or theoretical formula but can be experientially traced in our own experience; it is a process that happens thousands of times in a single day.

> What we contact we feel
> What we feel we perceive
> What we perceive we think about
> What we think about we proliferate about
> What we proliferate about we dwell upon
> What we dwell upon becomes the shape of our mind
> The shape of our mind becomes the shape of our world.

We are woken by an unexpected sound in the night; it startles us and registers as unpleasant. We identify it as a squeaking floor board. We begin to wonder and speculate about what it is. Perhaps it is an intruder. We keenly listen out for the next creak of the floor, and our mind begins to be shaped by anxiety. We are convinced we are being burgled, living in a dangerous world. We find the courage to turn on the light and soon realize the sound is that of a branch scraping on the window, blown by the wind, and our world of the moment changes. The process of shaping and constructing our world is a continuous process, sometimes benign and at times catapulting us into terror, aversion, and contractedness.

Equanimity, coupled with mindfulness and curiosity, guides us to find the courage to question these constructed worlds, which are so easily given the authority to guide and determine our choices, acts, speech, and ways of responding. We become sensitive to the moments of contact, our sense doors meeting the world of sensory experience. We come to know the feeling tones as they register, the pleasant and the unpleasant, and hold those feelings in mindfulness. We begin to notice when our thoughts begin to proliferate and our minds begin to obsess and dwell in the thoughts that are shaping our world. We learn it is possible to track this process without becoming lost or overwhelmed. We may even use a few simple phrases to remind ourselves.

May I rest in not knowing.
May I find ease in stillness.
May I be equally near all things.

The process of superimposing perceptions and its history of association upon anything or anyone is a process of constructing a world of finiteness out of life, which is fluid, dynamic, and ever changing, a life that asks for a fluidity of responsiveness rooted in our capacity to see all things, all people, and ourselves anew. The deepening of our understanding is a movement toward the infinite. We can perceive and navigate our way through life, but the link between perception and the tendencies toward greed, hate, and confusion is severed. It is this severance that liberates the world, other people, and others from our definitions and views. Seeing all things anew, our responsiveness is rooted in immeasurable kindness, compassion, joy, and equanimity, which are as boundless as life itself. Free of the prisons of views, we abide in a fluid, unfolding world that has no center.

In one of the early texts of the Udana Sutta, titled "In Praise of Equanimity," the Buddha taught,

For one who clings motion exists
But for one who does not cling
There is no motion
Where there is no motion, there is stillness
Where stillness is, there is no craving
Where no craving is, there is neither coming or going
Where no coming or going is
There is no arising nor passing away
There is neither this world, nor a world beyond, nor a state
    between.
This verily is the end of suffering.

Equanimity, born of understanding, teaches to abide in stillness, the deepest peace. It is the stillness of wakefulness, alive and responsive to life. The roots of reactivity and suffering—in greed, ill will, and delusion—are brought to an end. The reification of "self" and "other" through confusion and distorted perception becomes transparent. The heart is freed from the finiteness born of confusion and reactivity. It is a stillness of freedom imbued with kindness, joy, and compassion. Equanimity is the deepest peace, a boundless freedom possible for each of us. The Buddha taught: "If I did not think this path and its fruition in liberation was possible for you, I would not ask it of you. Because I know this path of immeasurable freedom is possible for you, therefore I ask it of you."

Conclusion

An Awakened Heart, an Awakened Life

I TEACH JUST ONE THING, THERE IS DUKKHA AND THERE IS
THE END OF DUKKHA.
—The Buddha

At the heart of all of the Buddha's teaching there lies a singular message—an awakened heart, unshakeable liberation is the goal of the path. The Buddha was little interested in metaphysical debate or transient transcendent experience. When he got up from the bodhi tree on the eve of his awakening, he went forth into the world, guided by compassion, to encourage others to come to the same liberating insights he had come to understand. Freedom, he taught, was firmly rooted in the ground of integrity. Our mind could be trained to be a reliable friend, free of proliferation and confusion. Our heart could abide in immeasurable kindness, compassion, joy, and equanimity. In this inner climate, profound insights would be revealed. An awakened heart is embodied in an awakened life, imbued with mindfulness, care, and respect.

Dukkha, the Buddha taught, is to be understood. Dukkha is a nuanced world; too often it is simplistically translated as "suffering," but it embraces the entirety of the human condition. As embodied human beings we are all asked to understand our relationship to the frailty of living in a body. As changing human beings we are asked to understand our relationship to all the changes that touch our lives. As human beings interwoven with a world that is unpredictable and uncertain, we are asked to understand our relationship to uncertainty. The end of dukkha that the Buddha spoke of is clearly not a magical formula for achieving immortality or devising a body that will not be subject to all the afflictions that a body can experience. The end of dukkha is not found through futilely endeavoring to overcome the reality of impermanence and instability. The end of dukkha taught by the Buddha is the cessation of psychological and emotional distress born of confusion. It is the ending of greed, hatred, and delusion. Nibbana, or liberation, as taught by the Buddha, is a process of unbinding the heart from the distortions, fears, and clinging that bind us to struggle and anguish. Dukkha can end, and a life of freedom and wakefulness can be lived. The Buddha's teaching on suffering and the origins of suffering lives alongside the teaching of unshakeable liberation. The teachings on the potential of the human heart to flounder in great distress and sorrow live alongside the teachings of the potential of every human heart for immeasurable kindness, compassion, joy, and equanimity.

Even though we intellectually acknowledge the vulnerability of our body and our mortality, we find ourselves in denial, fear, and rejection of this truth. Even as we nod our heads in agreement with the reality of impermanence and the instability of conditions we cannot control, it is deeply challenging for us to live in the light of what we know. A world of distress is born of the ongoing argument we have with the unarguable. This argument is what we are invited to understand, deeply and profoundly. An awakened heart and an awakened life are lived in the light of what we know. Learning to release our arguments with the unarguable is the greatest act of compassion we can offer to ourselves and to the world.

The great genius of the Buddha was to root his teaching in what each of us already knows or has glimpsed, even if only briefly, in our lives. What is it that we know? We know about impermanence— our whole life has been teaching us this unarguable truth. We see it reflected in the seasons of the year, the seasons of our lives, in all that we cherish and all that we fear and dislike. We know about uncertainty and instability—all the ways our world can crumble in a moment. We know about pain—all the ways our bodies can suffer. With only a little investigation, we come to know that "self" is not a noun but a verb, an endlessly changing process shaped by conditions and by what is being identified with in the moment. We know that to live in a world governed by craving, fear, and aversion has only one outcome—more sorrow, defensiveness, alienation, and ill will. We know the power of generosity—the small and large acts of generosity, given and received, that ennoble our lives. We know the power of mindfulness to awaken our world inwardly and outwardly. That mindfulness allows us to live wholeheartedly, protects our hearts, and opens the door to profound understanding. We know the power of kindness and compassion to heal alienation and division. We know that grasping and clinging lead only to agitation and contractedness, imprisoning us in a contracted and fearful world. We know the freedom of not clinging. We know the value of inner stillness, a calm abiding that is the ground of listening and empathy. We know that genuine joy and happiness are inwardly generated, that there is nothing that can be gained that can truly gladden a discontented heart. We know that we are interconnected: none of us stands alone; our very life relies upon the lives of many. Perhaps the most significant knowing we discover is that we have the freedom of choice. Mindfulness illuminates our world of experience and the ways that our personal world is being born and shaped moment to moment. In that illumination we can track the construction of a world of distress. With mindfulness we equally begin to sense the ways we can cultivate the qualities of heart that lead to the end of distress. We can choose what pathways we walk on and how our world of the moment is shaped.

With an awakened heart and an awakened life, we live in the light of what we know and deeply understand, embodying and manifesting our knowing in boundless kindness, compassion, joy, and equanimity. Yet we encounter disappointing moments when we sense the dissonance between our knowing and how we live, see, act, and think. We wish to live with generosity yet find ourselves fearful of deprivation, holding tightly to all that we call "mine." We intend to live with as much kindness and compassion as possible in our meeting with the world yet seem to fall so easily into irritation and intolerance. We commit ourselves to mindfulness yet are so easily captivated by habit. We long for calm and stillness, yet agitation and restlessness visit us more often than we would wish. Dissonance is uncomfortable; aware of the gap between our aspirations, values, and deepest intentions and the lived realities of our lives, we are prone to judge ourselves for our imperfections or fall into despair.

Dedicated to awakening and being a conscious participant in the awakening and healing of our world, we approach dissonance differently. We understand this is the very classroom of our learning and awakening. This is where we deeply inquire into what is sabotaging and undermining the intentions we have to live an awakened life and binds us to forgetfulness. The Buddha was committed to understanding the anatomy of distress, knowing the end of distress could be born only of understanding. The chaos, confusion, and struggle so familiar to us is not a life sentence but created and re-created through confusion, one moment at a time. Understanding for ourselves the anatomy of confusion, we can dispel it one moment at a time. Learning to liberate this single moment from struggle is a building block of coming to know the end of all confusion and a liberated heart.

The Buddha identified four primary roots of confusion and struggle. The first is the tendency to seek and see permanence in a life that is purely process—fluid, dynamic, and changeable. The second is to see the beautiful in that which is not implicitly beautiful. We posit the capacity to deliver happiness in that which cannot yield enduring happiness and find ourselves enchanted not only with the world of objects, but with our own fantasies about the happiness those objects, events, and experience will deliver. The third is to see that which is unsatisfactory as being satisfactory. Stripped of confidence and aspiration we resign ourselves to a world of confusion and despair marked by transient moments of pleasure. The fourth is to see an independent self in all things. The tendency to reify and define ourselves by changing phenomena and to invest an independent self-existence in all things occurs in each moment of clinging. The Buddha suggested that as long as these distorted views remain unquestioned, there are in place all the necessary ingredients for the creation and re-creation of distress. These views, deeply embedded in our consciousness, are the fertile ground for craving, aversion, fear, and grasping to grow. They are the fuel of perpetuating all distress. In any moment of distress and struggle in our lives, we can learn to pause and examine the anatomy of that distress. We can learn to liberate our hearts, to relinquish our arguments with the unarguable and come to know what it is to live in the light of what we know—an embodied understanding. The deep, experiential investigation of the causes of distress is the primary ingredient for the ending of distress.

The Buddha taught numerous gateways to liberation. If the pathways of kindness, compassion, joy, and equanimity are to be immeasurable and lead to an unshakeable liberation of the heart, they need to be rooted in a profound understanding that is also unshakeable. The brahma viharas, cultivated skillfully, are both pathways to profound liberation and the embodiment of awakening. For these qualities to be pathways that lead toward liberation, they need to engage with the greed, hatred, and delusion that lead away from liberation. Each of the brahma viharas has what are called "near and far enemies."

The near enemy of metta or boundless friendliness takes the form of selfish affection, the kindness that we extend to those we love yet excludes those we struggle with or don't know. It is the limited and conditional kindness that looks for a return of affection in order for it to be sustained. It is the kindness that hinges upon people meeting our expectations and needs and that turns to coolness in the face of those needs being disappointed. The far enemy of immeasurable kindness is the painful ill will we can experience in the face of difficult people, or even lovely people when they are judged to have failed us. Conditional friendliness extends beyond the boundaries of our human interactions into all of the events and experiences that we attend to only when they please or gratify us. In the near and far enemies of genuine kindness we see lurking the threads both of ill will and craving that are deeply implicated in the creation and recreation of distress.

The near enemy of compassion is pity; its far enemy is cruelty, or the wish to see another harmed. Genuine compassion teaches us to turn toward pain and sorrow, to feel it in our bones and to respond with care and the commitment to healing sorrow. Even when we know it is not possible to heal all of the afflictions in this world, we act as if it is possible to do so. Even as we know that greed, hatred, and delusion may be endless, we live as if it is possible to bring them to an end. Pity may look like compassion, yet it safely distances us from the rawness of pain. Feeling sorry for another may allow us to make gestures of help yet also excuse us from the empathy with another's suffering that may be deeply disturbing to us. Compassion welcomes that disturbance, balancing it with joy and equanimity, whereas pity fears intimacy with pain. In pity the sense of "self" and "other" is firmly established. In genuine compassion all notions of "self" and "other" become transparent. Cultivating compassion in the face of pain, we are learning to undo the reification of "selfing" that is built upon clinging and confusion.

In cultivating immeasurable compassion as the cornerstone of an awakened heart, we are asked to find the courage to uproot its far enemy—the impulse to harm another or ourselves through thoughts, words, or acts of harshness and cruelty. We begin to sense the fear that underlies harshness and meet the suffering of that fear with compassion. We sense the profound suffering, estrangement, and pain that are born of cruelty, or wishing harm upon another. We come to the same profound understanding that the Buddha discovered—that hatred will never be healed by hatred—and commit ourselves to the end of hatred through an embodied courage and compassion.

The near enemy of appreciative joy is exuberance; its far enemy is resentment. We love the vitality of exuberance and passion, yet in thrall to them we easily become forgetful. We find ourselves inclining to that which is seen to implicitly hold the power to enliven and animate us. The ground of craving is to externalize the sources of aliveness. We forget the quieter joy that is born of being fully present in this life that is asking for our attention rather than our consumption. We can easily become intensity addicts, chasing peak experiences in order to feel fully alive. Joy asks for stillness and receptivity; exuberance draws us into agitation. A liberated heart sees the end of all agitation.

The far enemy of boundless, appreciative joy is resentment. We look at the world and other people with a sense of deficiency and envy. Both deficiency and envy fuel aversion and craving, the toxic patterns that bind us to distress. In cultivating immeasurable joy we reclaim the sources of appreciation, contentment, and gladness that lie within our own hearts. We learn to lay down the burden of comparing, judging, and evaluating ourselves and others, knowing these serve only to fuel "self" and "other" constructs that are rooted in delusion. Appreciative joy is the home of the awakened heart; it can be discovered in all moments of our lives.

The near enemy of equanimity is indifference; its far enemy is clinging. Indifference is made possible only through numbness. Numbness is sought for when we feel helpless and fearful in the face of the magnitude of suffering in ourselves and in our world. Feeling unable to bear the pain around and within us, feeling ineffective in the face of the path of transformation and healing, we are tempted to seek sanctuary in indifference. A young child, faced with a family break-up and loneliness, confessed, "It is too painful to care." It can be deeply painful to care, yet care is asked for us in a world both of affliction and possibility. Deeply rooted in kindness, compassion, and joy, we have the resources within that allow us to care deeply yet not be overwhelmed by this conflicted world. Equanimity is our greatest strength in liberating our hearts from the extremes of craving and aversion. Equanimity is our greatest ally in turning toward a world scarred by craving and aversion.

Cultivating our capacity for boundless equanimity, we begin to uproot the tendency to cling to events and experiences, a tendency that is only a magnification of craving and aversion. Where clinging is, distress follows. Where clinging is, the isolated and limited "self" is born. This we begin to understand deeply, and we learn to stand in the midst of all things with unshakeable poise. We begin to sense the freedom born of no longer being enchanted by craving, aversion, and clinging. Equanimity is a moment-to-moment cultivation; its fruition is liberation.

Each of the brahma viharas has an affective element to it. The moments of unhesitating kindness we glimpse in our lives have an affective element of warmth and tenderness. Compassion brings forth the affective quality of deep care, connectedness, and responsiveness. Joy has an affective element of gladness, aliveness, and vitality. The affective element of equanimity is one of cool poise, balance, and steadiness. The glimpses we have in our lives of these qualities, often unsought and unexpected, reveal to us the possibility of each of us to know and trust these qualities in our hearts. The seeds of profound emotional maturity and freedom lie in each of our hearts. The seeds of emotional and psychological freedom that underlie a way of living our lives rooted in immeasurable kindness, compassion, joy, and equanimity are already present within us.

To bring the seeds of kindness, compassion, joy, and equanimity to fruition, we are asked to make a profound commitment to a way of being in this world guided by the intention to abide within this way of responding to life. The pathways of cultivating the brahma viharas are not endeavors meant to repeat and recapture an effective experience but are moment-to-moment opportunities to strengthen our capacity to meet each moment of our life with kindness, compassion, joy, and equanimity. Intention is the vehicle for this. In the midst of all events and experiences, we plant the intentions of kindness, joy, compassion, and equanimity. A Roman philosopher once said, "We dance through life, like puppets, on the end of the strings of our impulses." The commitment to kindness, compassion, joy, and equanimity guides us to a different way of being in this world, an intentional life that embodies all of the qualities that liberate the moment from fear and distress. It is suggested that the entire path of awakening rests upon the head of the pin of intention. The intention to be awake, the intention to speak, act, and think with kindness, compassion, joy, and equanimity is not something that is set just once. Before we act, speak, and engage with the world, we remember that in every moment we stand at a crossroads. We can follow the familiar and well-trodden pathways of the habits of aversion, mistrust, and craving, or we can set our hearts upon the pathways of awakening. We can learn to live an intentional life guided by insight and care.

The cultivation of the mind inclined toward kindness is dedicated to uprooting the toxic power of ill will. Through cultivating the intention to befriend all moments, all people, and all events, we learn the power of generosity, and we learn to care. The path of kindness protects our heart from the grip of aversion and is a guardian not only of our own hearts but of the world. Holding the intention to befriend all moments and people at the forefront of all our thoughts, words, and acts, we experientially discover that to change the shape of our mind of the moment is to change the shape of our world of the moment. We learn we can befriend not only the events and people in our lives, no matter how difficult they may be, but we can equally befriend the entirety of our own being, no matter how difficult we can be. The small moments of seeing our hearts shift from aversion to kindness inspire the possibility in this life to make kindness the home of our heart. What we frequently incline the heart toward becomes the inclination of the heart, guiding our thoughts, words, and acts.

There is an ancient teaching that encourages that "wherever our gaze may fall, may it be filled with kindness and respect." We learn to treat all moments with respect. We understand that everything matters. The teaching goes on to say: Do not take lightly small expressions of ill will, believing they do little harm. Even a tiny spark can set a mountain alight. Equally do not take lightly small acts and words of kindness, believing they make little difference. The great oceans are filled by drops of water, one by one. Establishing the mind in a commitment to kindness teaches us the most deeply ethical way to live in this world. We become a good friend to ourselves and others—trustworthy, honest, and transparent.

Compassion is a dedication to understanding suffering and its causes and a commitment to its end. Compassion teaches us to forsake pathways of abandonment and denial. We learn we can be fearless in turning toward this difficult life. We learn in compassion much about forgiveness. Compassion teaches us not to blame, but to commit ourselves to uprooting the greed, hatred, and delusion that scar our world. We discover that compassion can be boundless and immeasurable, embracing all beings. Compassion shows us the way to be a friend to those who have no friend, a guardian of those in need of protection, and a light to those who are lost. There is no higher motivation or intention in this life than to have compassion, with its dimensions of empathy and responsiveness, at the heart of all that we do.

The cultivation of joy reveals to us how we have internalized the ideology of insufficiency and lack. It offers deep insight into the roots of the craving that can govern our lives and the ways we can learn moment by moment to return to a genuine sense of inner sufficiency. Contentment, appreciation, and peace can be the home of our hearts. Joy teaches us to release the comparing and judging mind that repeatedly highlights and deepens the reification of "self" and "other." The understanding born of cultivating of joy releases the mind from the contracted prisons of want and separation.

All of the noble abidings have the effect of calming the voice of "self." Equanimity has at its heart a profound understanding of nonself. There is the cessation of "I" and "you," "self" and "other," "mine" and "yours." The ground of all confusion is dissolved; greed, hatred, and delusion can come to an end in this very life. Equanimity, imbued with kindness, compassion, and joy, becomes unshakeable, and we know a heart that is awakened. The heart is awakened and liberated by understanding suffering and its causes. The heart is liberated through the cessation of greed, hatred, and delusion. The noble abidings of kindness, compassion, joy, and equanimity becomes immeasurable and unshakeable when rooted in profound understanding. Step by step and moment by moment, a home is established in the qualities that ennoble our lives and hearts and offer a life of wakefulness. In this fragile life, so easily broken and riven by affliction, we come to see that it is only kindness, compassion, joy, and equanimity that make sense. As the Buddha put it, "Whether standing, sitting, walking or lying down we abide in kindness, compassion, joy, and equanimity. There is no more noble way to live in this world." This is the essence of a liberated heart, rooted in unshakeable kindness, compassion, joy, and equanimity.

Notes

INTRODUCTION:
THE LANDSCAPE AND EMBODIMENT OF LIBERATION

1. John Peacock, trans., Singhalese text, *Singhalese Pirit Book*. This is a chanting book of blessing used by monastics. It is not published but the passages in a Pirit book are often drawn from the Pali Canon (in this case unidentified).

CHAPTER 1. IMMEASURABLE KINDNESS

1. John Peacock, trans., The Mettā-Sutta (Karaniya mettasutta, Sutta Nipata 143–52), 2016. Unpublished.
2. Patrul Rinpoche, *The Words of My Perfect Teacher: A Complete Translation of a Classic Introduction to Tibetan Buddhism,* trans. Padmakara Translation Group (San Francisco: Harper San Francisco, 1994).
3. Ven. Narada Thera, trans., The Dhammapada (London: John Murray, 1954).
4. Santideva, *A Guide to the Bodhisattva Way of Life,* trans. Vesna A. Wallace and B. Alan Wallace (Ithaca: Snow Lion Publications: 1997). Also in Geshe Sonam Rinchen, *The Thirty Seven Practices of Bodhisattvas: An Oral Teaching,* trans., Ruth Sonam (Ithaca: Snow Lion Publications, 2001).
5. Bhikkhu Bodhi, *The Connected Discourses of the Buddha: A Translation of the Samyutta Nikaya* (S.47:19) (Somerville: Wisdom Publications, 2000).
6. John Peacock, trans., Mettā-Sutta, 2016. Unpublished.
7. Bhikkhu Nanamoli and Bhikkhu Bodhi trans., *The Middle Length Discourses of the Buddha: A Translation of the Majjhima Nikaya* (Somerville: Wisdom Publications, 1995).
8. Bhikkhu Nanamoli, trans., *The Path of Purification,* Buddhaghosa (Sri Lanka: Buddhist Publication Society, 1979).
9. John Peacock, trans., Mettā-Sutta.

CHAPTER 2. COMPASSION

1. Richard Selzer, *Mortal Lessons: Notes on the Art of Surgery* (Orlando: Harcourt Brace, 1996).
2. Santideva, *A Guide to the Bodhisattva Way of Life.*

CHAPTER 3. JOY

1. Ve. Narada Thera, trans., The Dhammapada.
2. Oliver Sacks, *A Leg to Stand On* (New York: Touchstone, 1984).

3. Longchen Rabjam, "Finding Comfort and Ease in Meditation on the Great Perfection" in Dalai Lama XVI, *Mind in Comfort and Ease: The Vision of Enlightenment in the Great Perfection,* ed. Patrick Gaffney, trans. Matthieu Ricard, Richard Barron, and Adam Pearcey (Somerville: Wisdom Publications, 2007), 227–252. Also in Herbert V. Guenther, *Kindly Bent to Ease Us, vols. 1–3* (Berkeley: Dharma Publishing, 1975–76).

CHAPTER 4. EQUANIMITY

1. Maurice Walshe, trans., *The Long Discourses of the Buddha: A Translation of the Digha Nikaya* (Somerville: Wisdom Publications, 1995).
2. John Peacock, trans., Eighteenth-century Sinhalese Pirit, or chanting book of blessings. Unpublished.